Five Nights at Freddy's™

RETURN TO THE PIT

AN INTERACTIVE NOVEL

BY
SCOTT CAWTHON
ADRIENNE CRESS

SCHOLASTIC INC.

Special thanks to DJ Sterf

ISBN 978-93-5954-975-0

Book design by Jeff Shake

This reprint edition March 2025

Printed in India at Shivam Offset Press, New Delhi

Intro

This town. This stupid, pointless town. You know how when you look at a map all you see is a dot and a name of a place? Well, that's this town up close. Just a dot with a name. Your name is Oswald, you're a ten-year-old fifth grader, and you hate it here. This town is just plain terrible. You didn't always think this. You assumed that every kid kind of hated the town they grew up in. That everyone got bored with the same old, same old. That's just life. But then you realized, oh no, this town, this town in particular? *This* town? It's the *worst*.

And it's not just your opinion. It's an objective truth. After all, if others actually liked it here, then maybe the majority of the stores along Main Street wouldn't be all boarded up. Maybe people would want to stay and work here. Maybe your best friend wouldn't have moved away because his parents wanted a "better life" for him.

Yes. This is the kind of town people run away from. A couple years ago when there was a games shop and even a movie theater, maybe people would have stayed then. But now? Now you'd better run away fast from it! Run away and never look back!

But not you. Not your family. No, your family has been here for generations and Mom has a good job at the hospital, even if the hours are long and she always looks tired. So evidently that means you're stuck. Because no one in the history of time ever changed their mind about a thing.

- **IF YOU WANT TO PLAY ON *EASY* DIFFICULTY, ADD A PAIR OF <u>*YELLOW BUNNY EARS*</u> AND <u>*HALF OF A FAZBEAR COIN*</u> TO YOUR INVENTORY AND TURN TO PAGE 2.**
- **IF YOU WANT TO PLAY ON *NORMAL* DIFFICULTY, START OUT WITH ONLY YOUR WITS AND TURN TO PAGE 2.**
- **AT ANY TIME, YOU CAN TURN TO THE BACK OF THIS BOOK FOR SOME LINED PAGES IF YOU NEED TO MAKE NOTES FOR YOURSELF.**

It's the start of summer vacation and you're sitting in the car with your dad, looking out the window, staring at the buildings passing by. You notice the dead possum is still there . . . getting nicely cooked in the heat. Yum. It's a sunny day, but even a sunny day in this town is gloomy, painful. The storefronts are bleached from the sun, everything reflecting a white-hotness that makes you squint. The wood on the boarded-up windows are covered in graffiti tags, the glass of the few stores that still exist are dusty and dull. It all makes you feel kind of itchy.

You look down at the notebook in your lap instead. At the drawings you've made. Because you like to draw. Or at least you *think* you like to draw. Drawing is a way to escape the mundane, the repetition every day, the droning on of teachers who have to give the same lesson over and over so everyone understands even if you got it already. But would you do it if you didn't have to use it to survive? You don't know. You think you would.

You think you like it.

You're pretty good at drawing. And lately you've gotten into sketching these animal characters that are kind of like mascots. One's a bear. One's a bird. One's a rabbit. They play in a band. Yeah, okay, super cheesy, and a little childish but, whatever.

Everything's so whatever.

"Excited that school's finally done?" Dad asks. He's been trying to make pleasant small talk since you left home to go to the library. You've been ignoring him. He had put on one of his favorite country music stations that plays the worst kind of music and the only way to survive was to pretend you couldn't hear it. But now he's trying to talk to you.

And you ignore him again.

Because honestly? The truth is the answer isn't that easy. Yes, it's great to be done with another year of school, to be going into middle school finally next year. Sixth grade feels like a serious step up. But also . . . you're pretty much doomed to spend this summer completely and utterly alone.

Your best friend Ben's not here. He left for the good life in Myrtle Beach. And it's not like the other kids at school want to hang. Nah, they'd rather just call you "Oswald the Ocelot" or even better, "Lee Harvey Oswald" after the guy who killed the president back in the '60s. Why do popular kids pick on the unpopular ones? It feels like such a waste of time for them. Don't they have anything better to do? Why can't they just leave you alone like they do most of the time?

And Mom works crazy long hours as a nurse at the hospital, and Dad's work shifts start early in the morning, so it's not like even if you wanted to be that kid who hangs with his parents you could even do that. So there's no one to hang out with, and it's not exactly like your parents have any extra money so that you could do anything cool. Again, your big plans today are going to the library. The very free library.

Does Dad really want to talk about all that?

But now you feel kind of bad ignoring him so much so you push out an answer: "It's whatever."

Dad sighs. He's probably over you just like you are over him. You wouldn't blame him. "I know it's tough without Ben."

"It's tough without anything! I hate being poor." You probably shouldn't have said that. There are people out there way worse off than you. But you're frustrated and it's too sunny out. Too stinging bright.

"We aren't poor, Oswald," your Dad says with another sigh.

"Yeah, I know."

"And I just got the new job at the deli and I'm pretty sure I'm getting a promotion soon. Things are looking up, I promise!"

Why was Dad always so hopeful? You'd think the longer you lived in this town, the less hope you'd have. You'd think it would all just slowly seep away. Like a leaky faucet, just *drip drip drip* down the drain.

"Sure." You look at your sketch of the singing bear. His eyes kind of freak you out even though you drew them in the first place.

"Hey, I have an idea," Dad says.

Dad usually has plenty of ideas. Not always good ones.

"Why don't you go to Jeff's Pizza after you're done at the library. Get yourself a soda and a slice? How does that sound? Could be a new summer tradition."

It sounds a bit like bribery. Like he's trying to make you think a piece of pizza is as amazing as a summer at the beach.

It also kind of sounds okay. After all, pizza is your favorite food.

- OKAY, WHATEVER, AT LEAST IT'S SOMETHING TO DO, AND PIZZA TASTES GOOD. IF YOU AGREE WITH HIS PLAN, TURN TO PAGE 5.
- A PIECE OF PIZZA ISN'T GOING TO MAKE EVERYTHING BETTER. AND YOU DON'T WANT DAD TO THINK HE CAN JUST BRIBE YOU WITH ONE. IF YOU SAY YOU AREN'T INTERESTED, TURN TO PAGE 23.

"Yeah okay, pizza sounds cool." You try to sound indifferent, like it doesn't matter. But your stomach rumbles right on cue, loud enough that Dad laughs. *Thanks so much for that, traitorous stomach.*

"Great! I love it when a plan comes together!" That's something Dad likes to say because there's an old TV show where someone said that all the time. Dad likes old TV shows and films. You guys watch old science fiction movies together all the time. Some of his favorites are the old Japanese kaiju movies where it's super obvious the monsters are actors wearing rubber suits. Which is kind of fun sometimes. Okay, so maybe you kind of like old things, too.

You pull up in front of the library. It's easy for Dad to stop the car on the street because no one's around. There's never anyone around in this town. Why you even have that single traffic light is anyone's guess. Like two cars travel by an hour.

Dad hands you cash for the pizza and you mumble a quick thanks. You just need to get out of the car even if it means going into the library. You slam the door behind you a little too loudly—you didn't mean it to seem that aggressive. You glance up, but Dad just waves happily at you and you don't feel guilty anymore.

You dash inside the library before you can feel any more feelings.

It's not actually the worst thing being at the library, it's more the principle of it all. Like you should be with Ben, hanging out, gaming and stuff, but instead you are on your own. Hanging out. And gaming and stuff. But the library is dark and air-conditioned, and they have this comic book series you've been working your way through. And when that gets boring you can also draw more of your mascot characters.

It's kind of okay, actually.

And the time passes faster than you expect, and suddenly you are back out in the bright sun. But even that's a bit better because it's lower in the sky now. And you make your way over to Jeff's Pizza. One of the few shops in town that's not boarded up.

Jeff's Pizza has always been a little creepy. But they do make good pizza, so you put up with the weird, dank smell and the strange shadowy figures that were painted over on the far wall, but you can kind of still see their lumpy outline. There's this raised platform in the corner, a stage once upon a time, maybe? It's super random. The booth benches are covered in this kind of plastic that sticks to your legs when you sit down. And even though you've seen Jeff himself wipe down the tables, you are pretty sure the rag he does it with hasn't been washed since the '90s.

And then there's the weird ball pit in the far corner. It's roped off with this kind of netting stuff and there's a hand-lettered sign that reads OUT OF BOUNDS, but why does it exist in the first place? Why have a dusty weird ball pit in the corner of a pizza place? And especially why if you don't want anyone to use it? It's not like you're super tempted by it, it kind of looks smelly and gross. But . . . you're not *not* tempted.

"Okay, kid, what'll it be?" Jeff himself. Greasy skin, greasy hair, grease on his apron.

"A plain slice and a Coke, please," you say.

Jeff nods and turns like he's got better things to do. Even though the place is empty and there are no other customers.

He brings you your slice and soda pretty fast and you inhale it just as quickly. Your stomach is still gurgling. Yeah, one slice is seriously not enough. You glance at your phone. Twenty minutes until Dad comes to pick you up. Now what? Sitting here surrounded by the smells of melted cheese and buttery crust is a special kind of torture. *Just focus on the dank smell*, you tell yourself, *inhale the dank.*

"Hey, kid. I've got extras, do you want?" Jeff is there in front of you in all his greasy glory with two slices of pepperoni in his hands.

Do you want? What kind of question is that?

"Uh, I don't have enough cash . . ."

"On the house, kid, we close early tonight. Need to get rid of the extras." He doesn't wait for you to say yes; he can clearly tell that's the answer. He walks off again in that strange way he does and you don't hesitate, you inhale the slices as well. So, so, so good.

Yeah, okay, maybe Dad's plan isn't terrible. Maybe you can do this again tomorrow.

Or maybe, like with everything else, it'll start to get boring. And it's not like you'll get free slices every day. And one slice isn't enough and just kind of feels disappointing.

- **NAH, IT'S BEEN PRETTY FUN. AND WHAT ELSE DO YOU HAVE TO DO, ANYWAY? IF YOU STICK WITH THE LIBRARY-FOLLOWED-BY-PIZZA PLAN TOMORROW, TURN TO PAGE 8.**
- **YEAH, YOU'RE OVER IT. IF TOMORROW YOU'RE JUST GOING TO VISIT THE LIBRARY, TURN TO PAGE 12.**

Dad is a little too thrilled how well his whole library-and-pizza idea went. You roll your eyes but he's not watching—he's just keeping his eyes on the road. Like there'd be anyone to crash into. He could probably do that thing they do in movies, where the driver just starts talking to the passenger and looking right at them, and still make it all the way home safe and sound.

As it is, you do make it home safe and sound and Dad suggests watching one of those old, terrible, but also kind of fun monster movies he likes. That you maybe like, too. Maybe. Just a bit.

"Oh, come on!" you say, pointing right at the screen, "you can basically see the guy's head inside the monster's mouth on the costume!"

"That's what makes it awesome," Dad replies with a laugh.

Another eye roll. This time Dad sees. Suddenly you're beaned in the face with a couch pillow. You can't help but laugh. "It's so cheesy."

"Nothing wrong with cheesy," replies Dad.

You shake your head but you don't stop watching the movie or anything. Because of course you do have to see if the mech lizard is going to defeat the giant zombie butterfly or not.

You finish the movie, you go to bed, you wake up and smell pancakes.

Pancakes are always a nice smell to wake up to.

"Morning, hon," Mom says as you slouch your way into the kitchen. You're still tired, but you have an exciting full day of going to the library ahead of you so you better be up and ready for it. Wow, you're even sarcastic to yourself inside your brain.

"Hey, Mom." You sit at the table and she gives you a peck on the top of your head while placing a plate of pancakes in front of you.

"How was yesterday?" she asks, passing you the syrup and then turning back to the stove.

"It was fine." Because it was. That's kind of all it was, really. It existed. It happened. That's about all anyone could say about it. Okay, the pizza was pretty good, but that's kind of pathetic to choose as some kind of exciting highlight.

"Well, I'm glad it was at least not terrible," Mom says.

Yeah, at least not that.

And then you get ready for another not-terrible day. The same old, same old. Reading more of that comic series. Eating more free pizza. Evidently Jeff has a ton of pizza just lying around or something. Maybe he should stop making so much? Well, you're not going to suggest anything to him while he's handing you the extra slices.

And then Dad picks you up and then it's the same cycle over and over again. Day after day. You run through that one comic series and start another. Your mascot band is now on tour, and you draw them in locations around the world. The pizza still tastes good but maybe it's getting a little boring?

Day after day.

At the end of the week there's a bit of a change in routine with "family night." Family night is a weekly tradition that you do with both your parents. Probably something to do with bonding, or whatever. It's just the three of you, it's not like you invite long-lost relatives or anything. It seems a little silly since you see your parents every single day. But yeah, it's true, the three of you hanging out together is not easy to do with your parents having such opposite work schedules. Anyway, family night can consist of anything, a board game or maybe a walk to get ice cream. Tonight it's a movie night, which is okay. But you're just kind of over everything at this point, including movies.

"Not excited about the movie, Oswald?" asks Dad, flipping through titles on the app.

You shrug. "I'm just kind of over everything. Nothing ever changes. It's the same every day. I wish we had money."

"Money isn't the most important thing," Mom says softly from her chair.

Yeah, yeah, you know that—she says that a lot. "It's not, but it makes things less boring." And even though you know you shouldn't say it because it'll make Mom sad, you add, "I hate this summer. It's so stupid. I don't want to watch a stupid monster movie."

"But you like monster movies," Dad says.

"Too much of anything is dumb. I just want to do something different, hang out with kids my own age. Not, like, my parents."

What's wrong with you? Why are you being so mean? Maybe you're just so over everything that you can't hold back all those angry thoughts in your brain. You're too tired to play nice.

"I know it's not what you want—"

"Yeah, because why would anything ever be what *I* want?"

"Lower your voice, young man."

"Why should I? I'm angry!"

"Because I'm your father, and I'm telling you to."

"Okay, you two, knock it off," says Mom with that trademark "Mom Voice" that just cuts through everything, even a fight, and makes everyone in the room shut up. "I'm serious. That's it, I'm making you both watch a rom-com."

The thing is, rom-coms are just as stupid as old monster movies, so what's the difference?

But also, you are just over hanging out with your parents. Being around anyone, really.

> **IF YOU GET UP IN A HUFF AND STOMP UPSTAIRS TO YOUR ROOM, TURN TO PAGE 13.**
>
> **YOU CROSS YOUR ARMS AND LEAN BACK INTO THE COUCH. IF YOU DECIDE TO WATCH THE ROM-COM, TURN TO PAGE 23.**

After you are done at the library, you walk home. You walk past Jeff's Pizza and the smells wafting toward you are pretty amazing, but you look at the rusty sign and the large boarded-up windows of the old expansion next door and know you've made the right choice. It's just all too depressing for words. And *definitely* too depressing to just go hang out inside there.

You continue your summer like this and the boredom seeps into every part of your life. You start picking fights with your Dad just to have something to do. The fights get worse and worse and they continue into the school year until you finally just start ignoring each other so you can get through the day. You realize you must have really upset Dad, because he always pushes you to talk about anything—even if you're really mean to him. But he's probably just as worn down as you are.

The idea of apologizing to him does occur to you, but it feels like too much effort. Besides, he should be the one to apologize to you first. He's the one who gave you this boring, stupid life. You continue to ignore him. Ignoring is easy and becomes a habit fast. It bleeds into the next summer. Into the next year. It takes you into high school. You continue to barely acknowledge each other as you grow up. Eventually you move out and leave town as soon as you can escape it. You try to answer the odd Dad text but you just don't care anymore. It's so much easier not to care. Eventually you lose touch completely. There comes a day when it is the last time you ever communicate with him.

GAME OVER

>TO TRY AGAIN TURN TO PAGE 2

Fine, you'll stay and watch the stupid rom-com. It'll be a good distraction, and also you feel a bit bad bringing Mom into all this. She was really looking forward to family movie night. So you sit down on the opposite side of the room from Dad at the end of the couch and start to watch. Cheesy music plays and there's a shot of a skyline of some big city—one that has so much stuff to do in it. Places to go, things to do and see. Adventures to be had. How are you jealous of some people in a rom-com? The first few scenes involve the main character and her friends hanging out. It just reinforces how totally alone you are. Why do people like watching these movies? They are way more depressing than tragedies.

As the story gets going you find it hard to focus. You aren't exactly jealous anymore, but you're also seriously not interested in whether Joanna from marketing will fall in love with the small-town hunk she went to prom with when she was a teenager. You find it laughable that she is so happy coming home to this tiny town after leaving the exciting big city. She seriously has no idea what she's in for. The same boring stuff, the same boring people. *Even the small-town hunk will get on your nerves one day,* you think, *trust me.*

You are so over all this. You can feel exhaustion seeping into you, like some outside force. Like the town itself is leaking into you. You don't exactly notice when you fall asleep, but it happens.

➤ TURN TO PAGE 23.

You fling open the door to your room and slam it hard behind you. You know you're not supposed to slam doors, and that's exactly why you do it. It feels good for a second, but then you immediately feel a little guilty. Not that guilty, just, you know . . . a little. You stomp over to your bed and fall hard onto it. Maybe a little too hard, as you hit your head against the wall, but you don't really care.

You pull out your phone to play a game and your stomach sinks. Looks like Ben has sent you a text: *Hey.*

Normally a text from Ben would make you feel happy and relieved, but you're not really in the mood to read all about his amazing time in Myrtle Beach while you live your weird *Groundhog Day*–like life of the library and Jeff's Pizza over and over again.

- **YOU SIGH. MAYBE IT WON'T BE TOO BAD. BESIDES, YOU COULD USE A DISTRACTION. IF YOU DECIDE TO TEXT BACK, TURN TO PAGE 14.**
- **YOU IGNORE THE TEXT AND PULL THE COVERS UP EVEN THOUGH YOU ARE STILL IN YOUR STREET CLOTHES. IF YOU FALL ASLEEP, TURN TO PAGE 23.**

Hey back, you reply. Then even though you really don't want to hear it you ask, *How's your summer?*

Ben tells you it's going great—he's been going to the beach and arcades. He's even made some new friends. The pit in your stomach makes you want to throw the phone across the room. Why is he telling you this? To make you jealous? He knows that he's abandoned you to the worst summer ever in the worst town ever. Feels kind of mean. But when he asks how your summer is going you have the ability to type out a short and nondescriptive: *Okay*.

You tell him about going to Jeff's. He tells you what you already know, that that place is seriously creepy.

You talk a bit about *War Rage 7* dropping this fall.

You say goodbye.

You stare at the ceiling.

Yup. As predicted, that whole conversation only made you feel worse. Awesome. You push your phone to the side and go to sleep. You dream a stupid dream where you're swimming at the beach with Ben and then your mascot band characters appear wearing floaties and try to drown you.

You wake up. You still feel like crap.

You know today is going to be just a crappy day.

"Look, Oswald, I'm sorry about last night. I can tell you're going through it," Dad says.

"Sure," you say. You don't believe it for a second. You also can't quite believe that you're back in the car, going to the library again. It's a living nightmare. No, not even a nightmare—it's too bleak for that. It's more like that feeling of zoning out when a teacher is talking for a bit too long. That bored, empty nothing where you're definitely not asleep but you're also not really present, either.

"I mean it, I want to say how impressed I am by you and how you've been handling this summer . . ."

"No," you interrupt him. You say it pretty loudly though you don't exactly shout it. Dad stops talking. He seems confused.

"You don't get to say that. It's not my choice. It's all yours. You don't get to be all Proud Dad when you're the reason my summer stinks."

"Oswald . . ."

"You could get a better job. We could move. There are things you could do, but *I* can't do anything. I'm just forced to be here. And that's not a good thing."

"Oswald, you know I'm up for a promotion . . ."

"You're always up for a promotion," you mutter under your breath, but of course Dad can hear it.

"And we can't just move. Your grandparents need us. Your mom's job is here. When you're a grown-up, you make commitments."

"Yeah, I know, for other people. Like your son."

You've pulled up to the library by now and it's such a good storming-off line that you make solid use of it by opening the car door in a huff and slamming it hard behind you as you leave.

The anger fuels you in a weird way for the day. It's not exactly fun, but at least you're not bored. When you find out the rest of the new comic series you were reading isn't out yet, you just use your anger to storm over to the computers. When the spinning wheel of death appears on the screen as you're trying to load your game, you just whip out your notebook in anger to draw instead. And when the bear starts looking like some kind of disintegrating monster and not the normal leader of your mascot band, you just lean into it and make it so his skin is peeling off, revealing a cold metallic structure underneath.

And when you finally get to Jeff's and have your slice, you eat the whole thing so fast you almost choke.

You sit there seething, waiting for Dad to pick you up. You really aren't ready to see him yet. You've done a really good job at keeping the anger going all day, though you are starting to feel a little tired now. Being furious is exhausting work.

You look around and see the ball pit in the corner. Yet another thing to be angry about! That stupid ball pit that no one is supposed to use, but somehow it still exists. What is the point of it? You glance over to look for Jeff, but he's disappeared into the kitchen.

This is your chance!

Your chance for what, exactly? Diving into a dusty ball pit probably covered in the sweat and snot and stuff from hundreds of kids over the years?

- **OH, WHO CARES ABOUT GERMS, AND NO ONE'S EVER DIED FROM GOING INTO A BALL PIT, SHEESH. IF YOU GO INTO THE PIT, TURN TO PAGE 18.**
- **YOU FEEL KIND OF GROSSED OUT AND DECIDE EVEN YOUR ANGER CAN'T PUSH YOU THAT FAR. IF YOU AVOID THE PIT, TURN TO PAGE 100.**

You stand up in the pit and notice you aren't alone. Little kids are playing in the dusty balls at your feet and you feel a little silly being surrounded by them. You smile awkwardly at a three-year-old who stares at you intensely as they try to shove an entire red ball into their mouth. Then you turn and climb out of the pit. You quickly walk away, pretending like you were never in it and look around some more.

This is truly incredible. You feel a buzzing of excitement, a feeling you didn't know you were still capable of feeling at all anymore. You feel happy. You wander over to the arcade games, which seem to extend into that shop next door to Jeff's. There are so many. There's Skee-Ball, there's Whac-A-Mole. There's pinball. Then there are all the actual arcade games, some of which you still play now on the computer. *Wrecking Crew. Road Blaster.*

It's hard to see the gameplay with so many kids surrounding each of the machines. Kids are waiting for their turn, placing tokens along the edge of the machines to hold their place. They cheer one another on and also sometimes chirp at one another, too. Everyone is just so energetic and hopped-up on sugary drinks and pizza and dessert.

It's simply wonderful.

You arrive at a game that no one is playing. There's no line or anything. You wonder if it's out of service or something but it's glowing and music is playing through the speakers. There's a pixelated yellow rabbit face smiling at you on the screen. Above it is the title, *8-Bit Escape*. At the coin slot there's a sign that reads: SPECIAL GOLD TOKEN ONLY.

➤ **IF YOU DON'T HAVE A SPECIAL GOLD TOKEN, TURN TO PAGE 26.**

➤ **IF YOU HAVE A SPECIAL GOLD TOKEN, TURN TO PAGE 24.**

You get up quickly and dash over to the pit. The rope is hardly an electrified fence or anything, and you step over it easily. You look into the pit. Up close you can see the dust on the colorful plastic balls, and you can smell . . . something . . . not great coming from its depths. Probably just stale like the rest of the pizza place. But you can't help but think of the word *rotting*.

There's no turning back now! Actually, you could totally turn back, it'd be super easy to do, but you are fueled by that anger and you are *determined*. Anyway, it's just a ball pit. What's the worst that can happen? You look over your shoulder one more time—Jeff is still in the kitchen, so you just go for it. And faster than you can think "pink eye," you jump into that pit and fall into a pile of dusty colorful plastic.

And keep falling.

And keep falling?

You are familiar with the story of *Alice in Wonderland*. You know all about the crazy deep rabbit hole. You think maybe you are suddenly somehow in her story—because this pit doesn't seem to have a bottom. You start to freak out and throw your arms wide to slow your fall. You need to do something quick! Maybe you can "swim" back to the surface? You kick your legs behind you and pull with your arms. Your hands scramble to use the plastic balls as leverage to pull yourself up, but you push them down beside you instead. Your heart is racing now, your feet flailing, your hands grasping, and now you're worried you can't breathe. No, don't be stupid, you're not actually underwater. There is air in here. There. Is. Air.

Slowly and painfully, you manage to "swim" back up through the balls. The higher you get, the more confident you are. You can do this, you can do this!

You *have* to do this!

With a *whoosh*, you finally pop your head out of the pit. You take in a deep breath and close your eyes in relief. There suddenly seems to be a bottom under you and you sit there trying to calm your speeding heart. Then you slowly sense something's different.

Something's off.

The sounds. The sounds you are hearing aren't the quiet drone of the old soda fridge behind the counter. They aren't of the faint muzak Jeff insists on playing, some kind of jazz flute awfulness. No, it's the clinking of bells, the laughter of kids, loud happy music, and . . . well, the sounds of joy?

You open your eyes.

And once again your breath is taken away.

You're still at Jeff's, or at least you think you are. The shape of the room, the general layout, seems like a perfect mirror to the restaurant you have now found yourself in.

No, wait, you're wrong. It's a little bigger, wider . . . you realize it's actually a perfect footprint of Jeff's Pizza and the shuttered shop beside it. Is this . . . Jeff's? If so, this Jeff's is twice as big.

This place isn't the creepy, musty pizza place you are familiar with.

This placc is *awesome.*

You stare at a crowded restaurant arcade. Kids are everywhere, laughing and playing games like the ones you'd heard Dad talk about from his childhood. These big cabinet-like games set up in rows, flashing colorful lights with big neon signs telling you what they are. So many games! You stare, wide-eyed and slack-jawed.

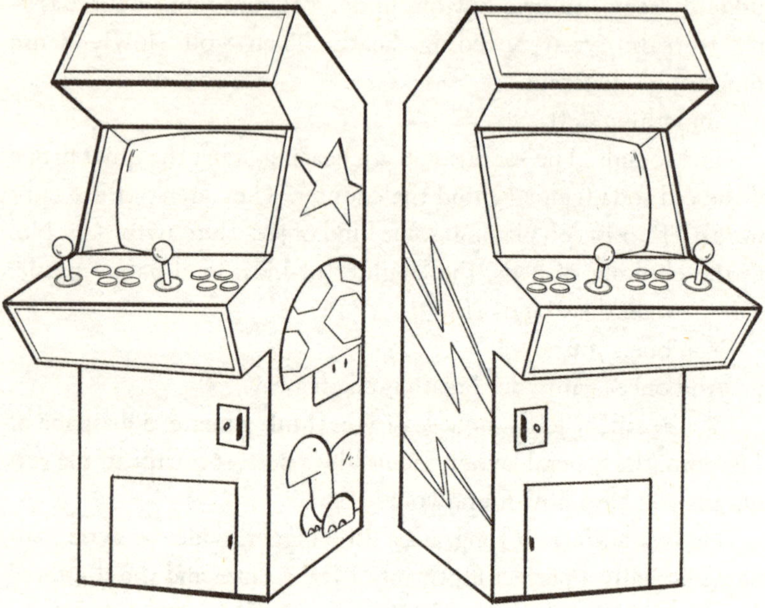

- THIS IS BEYOND AMAZING. IF YOU THINK YOU ABSOLUTELY NEED TO EXPLORE ALL THIS, TURN TO PAGE 17.
- IT DOESN'T MATTER HOW COOL IT ALL LOOKS, THIS IS ABSOLUTELY FREAKY AND WHO KNOWS WHAT MIGHT HAPPEN IF YOU STEP OUT OF THE BALL PIT. IF YOU NOPE OUT OF THERE AND DIVE BACK INTO THE PIT, TURN TO PAGE 30.

The time passes quickly when you actually have friends to hang out with and cool stuff to do. It also passes a little too fast because suddenly it occurs to you that you were supposed to meet your dad, like, an hour ago. You're already in the middle of a fight with him, and now he's going to probably be really upset with you for keeping him waiting.

That is, of course, if the ball pit is really some kind of wormhole that can predictably take you back to your time. What if it just sends you farther into the past? Or another dimension? Or maybe into the future? What are the rules, and what is the science behind magical ball pits? This is the stuff they really ought to teach you in school.

Speaking of pits . . . you get a really big one in your stomach. This awful sinking feeling. No, you can't freak out just yet. You can probably still get home, there's no reason not to assume so!

"Hey, guys, I'm sorry but I need to head out," you say. Then you worry about how to do that, exactly. Are you just going to say bye and then walk over and jump in the ball pit? That wouldn't seem weird at all.

But luckily Chip says, "Yeah, dude, us too. It was gnarly meeting you, man!" He sticks out his hand and you shake it again. You shake Mike's, too, and you watch as they walk out of the arcade together. Okay, well, that was good timing.

You quickly look around and no one is watching you. Except for that rabbit, but maybe it isn't even watching you. It's hard to tell what the mascot's eyes are actually focused on. It's like they are looking at everything and nothing at the same time.

You dash over to the pit and without any hesitation, you jump in. This time it doesn't feel like falling, you sink under the surface and wonder *What now?* Should you just wait? Should you pop up again right away? You decide to count to one hundred, as that's about how long you were swimming around in the ball pit in the first place probably.

You count, trying not to rush through it. And then when you hit a hundred, you quickly make your body pop back up again through the balls, into the restaurant.

Immediately everything is different, the smell, the sound, the dust. You're back! You're happy it worked, but also the awful depressing atmosphere that is Jeff's Pizza is such a stark contrast to the joyful one at Freddy's that you immediately feel a little disappointed. You look around for Dad, but he's nowhere to be seen. Did he think you bailed and went home? Oh man, you're going to be in so much trouble.

But that's when you look at the clock on the wall. It wasn't like you were paying close attention or anything, but it looks like not even ten minutes have passed. In fact, you're pretty sure the clock reads the same time as when you went into the pit.

Wait.

Does that mean time only passes in the pit world but not the real one? Does that mean you could hang out even longer with your new friends, play even more games, and just actually relax and have fun?

Is this something worth testing out, or were you just lucky this time?

- **HECK YEAH, IT'S WORTH TESTING OUT! IF YOU PLAN ON GOING INTO THE PIT AGAIN TOMORROW, TURN TO PAGE 32.**
- **NAH, NOT WORTH PUSHING YOUR LUCK. SPACE AND TIME AND WORMHOLES ARE HEAVY SCIENCE, AND YOU DON'T NEED TO BE MESSING WITH THAT. IF YOU'RE NOT GOING INTO THE PIT AGAIN TOMORROW, TURN TO PAGE 11.**

You have the strangest dream.

You are swimming in an ocean—maybe it's by Myrtle Beach, where Ben is. It's sunny and the water is a bright turquoise-blue. It's warm out and you feel so at peace. You are happy and content. Suddenly the skies go dark, and you hear a crash of thunder. The water has turned slate-gray, and the undertow suddenly grabs hold like a hand yanking you. It pulls you far out to sea. You struggle against it, dipping in and out of the waves and choking on the salt water, but the more you struggle, the farther away from shore you are taken. Then you realize you aren't in an ocean at all, but an enormous ball pit, just like that weird one in the corner at Jeff's. But this is a ball pit that goes on infinitely—there is no escape, no land in sight. You see it all as if you are looking down at yourself from above like a drone is filming you. You are tiny, surrounded by hundreds of thousands of colorful balls. The drone flies up farther and farther, revealing more and more balls. Millions upon millions. You are alone. It flies up farther and farther until you become indistinguishable from the balls. Your head is just another round object. You are going to drown in a colorful sea of plastic.

You wake with a start and quickly glance over at your parents who still seem engrossed in the movie. Your heart is beating fast. You know it was just a dream, but it feels almost like an omen . . . a warning.

On the screen, the marketing exec and the small-town hunk kiss, and you sink back into the sofa. You feel terrible and very uneasy. You decide then and there that you need to stay as far away from that ball pit at Jeff's as possible. And just to be safe, you'll stay as far away from Jeff's itself as possible. You decide you're never going back there ever again. And the next day you follow through with this decision.

➤ **TURN TO PAGE 11.**

You *do* have a gold token in your pocket for some reason! Weird! You grin as you pull it out and insert it into the game. You take a small step back as the game music starts playing and images flash across the screen.

Man, 8-bit. That classic '80s style of video game where all the images are made up of chunky pixels. It can be hard to tell what you're actually looking at. You know this because you've played a few versions of these old games on the computer. People are super nostalgic for them, so they remake them for newer consoles. You don't really get why. They are super old-fashioned.

Okay, yes, sometimes like all old things, they can be kind of fun.

The word "START" written in those classic big pixel letters flashes on the screen in front of you. You look down at the buttons on the arcade game and notice a little round joystick. You move it and the box around START lights up. You push the red button next to the joystick and the START turns a bright blue.

Suddenly the world whooshes around you. You stagger back and try to keep your balance as a tornado of color and blurred images spin faster and faster. What on earth . . . ? Are you about to time-travel again, perhaps even farther into the past? Will there be horses and carriages? Will there even be electricity? Oh man, what if there's no indoor plumbing?! You *so* aren't ready for this!

The whooshing stops.

You look around.

Well.

The good news is you're evidently still at Freddy's.

The bad news is . . . you're in an 8-bit version of Freddy's.

Yeah. That's right. The world has turned into some kind of video game–looking situation. And not a photorealistic modern video game. Nope, something totally out of the '80s, of course. You are now surrounded by a pixel version of the restaurant. Pixels making up arcade games, the booths, and the animatronic band in the corner. You look down, even the carpet under your feet . . . your feet . . .

Oh no.

Your feet are 8-bit.

You quickly hold up your hands. Yup, they are also 8-bit. And you figure if you looked in a mirror, your face would probably be, too. You're kind of glad there isn't one because you'd be tempted to look and you don't think you could handle seeing that.

You search around for someone, anyone, to call for help. But that's when you realize that while you might still be in Freddy's with all the usual Freddy's stuff in it, you are otherwise completely and utterly alone. There are no kids. No parents. No staff. Just you.

Alone in Freddy's.

In 8-bit Freddy's.

The full realization of your situation sits heavy on your shoulders and you take in a deep breath. Okay. Okay. This all happened when you pressed "START." Maybe there's a way to "stop"?

➤ TURN TO PAGE 31.

You shrug. It's okay, you don't need to play a game right now. What you need is to keep exploring because everything about this is insane. You wander back down the rows of arcade games, continuing to check out what everyone's playing, looking over the shoulders of the kids looking over the shoulders of the kid playing the game. It's so crowded in here. It's *amazing*! You wander back into the main part of Jeff's Pizza and it's then you notice those strange shapes painted over on the wall at Jeff's are visible! They are . . .

Well, they look like . . .

You furrow your eyebrows as you stare at them rising behind the wall of banquette seats filled with families eating pizza.

They look like your drawings.

A bear. A bird. A rabbit. All playing in a band. You take a step in to look closer. Below them, written in a colorful scrawl, is FREDDY FAZBEAR'S PIZZA. Okay, okay, so that's where you are. Not Jeff's. Not anymore. Or is this what it used to be? That's actually a good question. The games and everything suggest you're somehow in the past, but maybe you're in a different dimension?

Basically: You know where you are, but *when* are you? You look carefully at the people around you. You really examine them, looking for clues. You check their hairstyles, big and over-the-top, the girls with side ponytails, the boys' large and poofy. The clothes look different, too, lots of neon. Like seriously, a lot of neon. Too much neon, really, if anyone asked you, which they didn't. It's all old-fashioned and a bit funny. You grin.

Suddenly loud music blares. Much louder than the ambient music just playing around you.

You spin on your heels and find yourself staring at that platform. That old empty stage. Except now it isn't empty anymore. On it stands three life-sized versions of your drawings. In their band. They are playing a song together. Their movements are static and robotic and you realize these are animatronics programmed to move in sync as if they are really playing the music.

There's a group of little kids watching and laughing and wearing party hats. You're not really sure what's making them laugh like that. It's so obviously fake. And on top of that . . . it's kind of freaky. Those eyes, those creepy dead eyes that you couldn't stop drawing over and over again. They're way worse in reality than anything in your sketchbook.

Someone bumps into you and you wheel around. You're getting pretty dizzy with all this constant turning and trying to understand everything around you.

"Sorry, dude!" says a kid. He's about your age and he definitely has leaned into the whole poofy hair thing.

"Yeah, no, it's cool," you reply. Try not to stare, try not to stare. But you are *so* staring.

"You okay?"

You shake your head. Be normal, be normal. "Oh yeah, I'm fine."

"I'm Chip, and that's my friend Mike over there." Chip points to a tall kid with an Afro standing at the Skee-Ball game with a "Pizza Roller" decal on the side. "Haven't seen you here before."

You quickly come up with an excuse. "Oh yeah, I'm just visiting my grandma for a few weeks. This place is really cool. Love all these old games."

"Old games? Freddy's always has the latest games, that's why the lines are so epic."

"Yeah, no, I didn't mean like old as in old, I meant, like, old as in . . . cool." That wasn't a thing anyone said. That wasn't a saying in your time or theirs. Why did you say that?

But Chip nods and then shrugs. "Yeah, they are cool. Hey, you wanna play Pizza Roller with us?"

"Yeah!" Because you do. This might be some seriously

mysterious-ball-pit-travel-through-time-and-space situation, but the chance to actually play games with kids your own age and actually have fun? That would be amazing.

"You got a name?"

"Oswald," you reply. And you shake hands. Then quickly you head over to Mike who's holding the game for you.

You are not good at it. But they are taking it a bit easy on you at first as you figure out the mechanics. And sure enough after a few games they stop pulling their punches, and you even beat them a few times. You laugh at your first victory and high fives are had all around. You look across the room as Mike sets up for the next game. You know you're grinning like an idiot, but, man, it feels so good to just be happy for once. That's when you notice the person in the big yellow rabbit mascot costume standing in the far corner by some kind of back door. It's creepy, a lot like the animatronics onstage, but not as colorful—more like the costume has seen better days. It feels like the rabbit is staring right at you. But that's not possible, since there are so many other kids here. It's just the fake eyes, just one of those tricks where no matter where you are it looks like they are watching you.

Yeah.

Totally.

That.

- YOU ARE KIND OF MESMERIZED BY IT, EVEN THOUGH YOU KNOW IT CAN'T BE STARING RIGHT AT YOU. IF YOU DECIDE YOU NEED TO GO OVER AND CHECK IT OUT, TURN TO PAGE 36.
- IF YOU IGNORE THE RABBIT AND TURN BACK TO THE GAME, TURN TO PAGE 21.

You quickly dive back into the pit and decide to count to about a hundred (that's about the amount of time it felt like had passed when you did it the first time). Then you pop up again and thankfully you are back where you started. Okay, that was a crazy experience. Is the ball pit a time machine or a wormhole or something? You're okay not knowing the answer. You feel a huge sense of relief—then suddenly you are grabbed from behind! You look down at your chest in time to see a pair of yellow fuzzy arms, like a person wearing a mascot costume. You only have a moment to process the thought when you are pulled deep into the pit. Into that infinite pool where it's tough to tell which way is up. You kick and try to pull yourself away from the arms, but they are tight around you and you slowly surrender. You float in the pool of balls, the arms wrapped tightly around you.

They never let go.

You are now doomed to exist in the ball pit for all time.

GAME OVER

>TO TRY AGAIN TURN TO PAGE 2

You decide to explore the space. Where would a "Stop" button be hiding? It's weird, walking around an 8-bit world. Everything has hard edges, and you bump your knee against a table, wincing from the pain. You look down. A tiny square tear has appeared in your jeans. And also teeny-tiny red square dots. Is that pixel blood? Are you bleeding? Can you get injured here? Or worse?

Great, just great.

Just what you need. To be trapped is one thing, but being trapped knowing you can get hurt? That's another.

You swallow hard. Well, if you can, you can, and the only thing you can really do about it is to not die. You'll just have to avoid it.

Man, you hope you can.

You make your way over to where the ball pit usually is and instead you find a table set up as if it's ready for a birthday party. There's a cake at the far end of it and plates and cups placed at individual spots. But no one is sitting at the table.

And there is definitely no "Stop" button. And no "Pause" button, either.

You turn around. On the opposite side of the room, you notice an exit door to what you assume is some kind of hall. You approach it carefully. You've explored everywhere else in the space, so it probably makes sense to check it out. Then again, maybe you missed something back at the original arcade game itself. Maybe the "Stop" button is hidden there somehow?

➤ **IF YOU DECIDE TO EXPLORE THE BACK HALLWAY, TURN TO PAGE 42.**
➤ **IF YOU RETURN TO THE ARCADE GAME TO GIVE IT A CLOSER LOOK, TURN TO PAGE 37.**

You're still angry with Dad when he picks you up, but you are so distracted by this amazing new discovery you really don't have the energy to fight. You sit instead in silence as you ride home and go directly upstairs after dinner. You obviously can't fall asleep super early, but you hope you can soon because the sooner you sleep, the sooner it will be tomorrow, and the sooner you'll be back at Jeff's! Has anyone in the history of this town ever been excited to go to Jeff's before? Well, there's a first time for everything!

You do somehow manage to sleep and tomorrow does come. You follow your usual plan as always. It's so much harder to focus on playing an online game on the computer at the library when Freddy's awaits you!

And then you're at Jeff's! And then you've had your extra slices! And then . . . then you are alone with the ball pit. Quick as anything, you dash over and immediately jump into it. It doesn't seem so deep this time, nor does it seem quite so icky. The dust, the worries about pink eye, the smell . . . it kind of all doesn't matter as you count to one hundred. You cross your fingers and pop your head back up and find yourself in that Fazbear's place!

A wave of relief washes over you as you realize this is something that can be repeated, that you actually can have an amazing summer, that everything can be bright and cheerful and neon. This is huge. You try to see if Chip and Mike are anywhere, and while on the hunt you check out more of the games and the space. You even manage to catch a glimpse inside an office where a conveniently located wall calendar informs you it is the year 1985. That should be kind of terrifying to learn, but it's only all the more exhilarating! You're officially in the past! And it's *awesome*!

Chip and Mike find you, and you think it's pretty awesome to have people actually look for you! Chip's hair is sprayed and gelled into that perfect floof on his head, and Mike is wearing a

Back to the Future T-shirt. They grin at you, and of course you grin back.

"Hey, Oz!" says Chip.

"Oz?"

"You know, like in *The Wizard of Oz*? No one's ever called you that before?"

You think of all the names the kids at school have called you, none of them because they like you. All of them to upset you. But a proper nickname by people who like you . . . that's freaking amazing.

"They do now!" you say and your grin is so big your cheeks hurt. Going from no friends to friends who just gave you a cool nickname? Best. Summer. Ever. Uh, no offense, Ben.

"We ordered pizza, way too much, so you're sharing it with us!" says Chip. It's an order not a suggestion, and even though you've had your slices at Jeff's you are so not going to disobey such a tasty command.

As the three of you head over to Chip's booth, you notice that yellow rabbit still standing in its corner, just staring. How weird. And aren't mascots meant to circulate? Play with the kids? Do something more than just stand in one spot and stare?

Not creepy at all, yellow rabbit, not creepy at all.

The pizza arrives just as you sit down, and all three of you dig in.

"You know," Mike says between bites, "when I was little, I loved Freddy Fazbear's band. I even had a stuffed Freddy I used to sleep with. Now I look up at that stage and those things give me the creeps."

"It's weird, huh? How stuff you like as a little kid gets creepy when you're older?" Chip helps himself to another slice. "Like clowns."

"Or dolls!" adds Mike.

Or rabbit mascots, you think to yourself. But you don't say it because it's like neither Chip nor Mike have noticed it in the corner and that's a little weird. And you don't want to talk about anything weird.

The three of you do good work on the pizza and in no time at all you've finished it and are back in the arcade area. You feel kind of guilty as you head over to Skee-Ball that they've been paying for everything, but just as you arrive at the game you feel a weight in your pocket. You reach in and pull out a handful of game tokens! You glance in the pile to see if there's a golden one. No luck.

"Game's on me!" you announce, and the guys cheer.

You play Skee-Ball and then move on to air hockey, which you learn you are super fantastic at. So much so that you get top of the leaderboard and win a ton of prize tickets.

"Dude, you need to choose a prize!"

You nod and go over to the prize counter. Everything is kind of junk, but it's cool junk. There are a few things that catch your eye. The coolest and most practical thing is a flashlight, which you would actually totally use. Then there's a Freddy Fazbear action figure, which looks just like your drawing and could be a fun souvenir of your time-travel adventures. Last, there's a pair of yellow bunny ears.

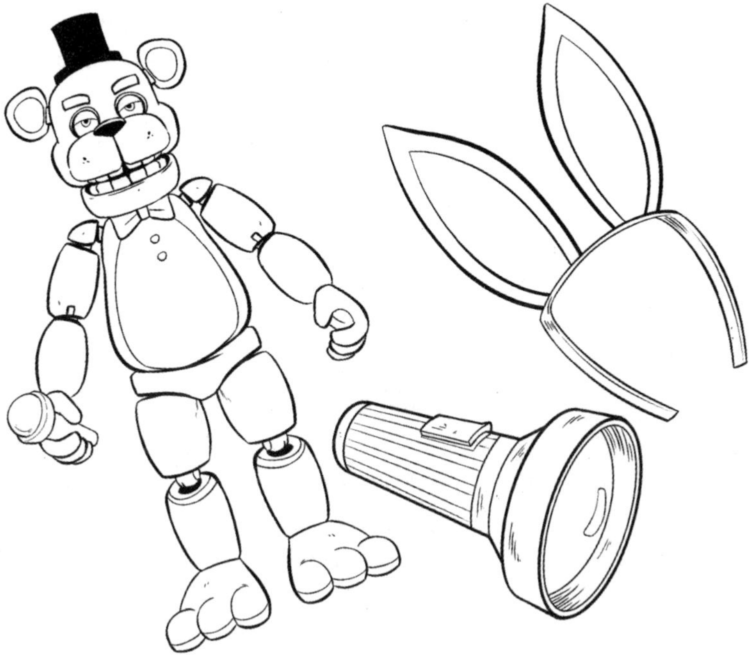

- IF YOU CHOOSE TO ADD THE FLASHLIGHT TO YOUR INVENTORY, TURN TO PAGE 105.
- IF YOU CHOOSE TO ADD THE FREDDY FAZBEAR ACTION FIGURE TO YOUR INVENTORY, TURN TO PAGE 38.
- YEAH, YOU HAVE RABBITS ON THE BRAIN. IF YOU CHOOSE TO ADD THE BUNNY EARS TO YOUR INVENTORY, TURN TO PAGE 40.

You walk over to the rabbit. You feel a little lightheaded, almost like you are strolling in a dream. All the kids making noise around you kind of vanishes in your mind, and your only focus is on the weird rabbit mascot. The eyes stay on you the whole time. You are drawn to them, even as they seem more dead and soulless as you get closer.

It's all so strange.

"Hi," you say when you arrive.

The rabbit doesn't say anything back.

What a weird mascot.

"So . . . you're a rabbit, huh?" It's a pretty stupid thing to say, but you're feeling kind of stupid. Kind of numb, honestly. Like there's this empty well inside you, but you are also inside it.

Okay, *that* was a trippy thought.

The rabbit produces one of those pointy party hats from behind its back. It's blue with blobs of green sparkles. An elastic dangles from the bottom.

You stare at it. What are you supposed to do with this hat, exactly? Does it want you to put it on? It's not your birthday! And you don't know anyone here except Mike and Chip, and they don't seem to be celebrating a birthday or anything. Besides, you can't even remember the last time you wore a birthday hat for anyone's birthday. They are kind of babyish.

You look back up at the rabbit. It still says nothing.

➤ **SOMEWHERE DEEP BEYOND THE WEIRD NUMB EMPTY FEELING, YOUR GUT TELLS YOU "NO." IF YOU BACK AWAY FROM THE RABBIT AND RETURN TO YOUR NEW FRIENDS, TURN TO PAGE 21.**

➤ **IF YOU TAKE THE HAT AND PUT IT ON, TURN TO PAGE 101.**

You turn around and there, standing before you, is a giant yellow 8-bit rabbit. Or . . . no. Not an *actual* rabbit. It's hard to tell because it's a pile of giant pixels, but somehow you understand that this isn't just some big bunny like in a cartoon, but someone wearing a mascot costume. You don't know why, but that horrifies you more than if it had been a cartoon bunny. Even though a giant bunny in real life is way weirder than just some person wearing a costume.

There's something ominous about this rabbit, though. Something not quite right.

As you try to figure out what isn't right about it, the rabbit opens its mouth wide. Wider than any mouth should open. You stare inside its gaping maw and see sharp teeth, or what you assume are sharp teeth—nothing can really be sharp-looking when it's all made of tiny squares. Huh. Weird.

You really should be more scared, you realize, when the rabbit lunges at you and pierces your flesh with the weird not-sharp teeth. You cry out, but the sound is more like a series of notes than a scream.

Everything fades to blackness.

A perpetual night.

Forever dead.

Until you regenerate back in front of the arcade game. You are a little dizzy and confused. It takes you a moment to realize what's happened.

Oh. I can't die. Or maybe you only have a certain number of lives? *But it's a game. I'm in a game*, you tell yourself.

The pain was real, though. You wince, remembering it. You're not sure how many times you want to be torn to shreds by an 8-bit rabbit mascot.

Well, you're back at the start now. And you still need to escape from this game. You really don't have much of a choice, so you might as well try again!

➤ TURN TO PAGE 31.

You hang with Chip and Mike a bit longer. They still want to talk movies, and you make a mental note of all of them so you can watch them at home when you get a chance. Eventually they have to leave and even though you feel like you could just hang out at Freddy's forever, you wait until they're gone and then head over to the ball pit.

Sure enough you pop back out in your own time, and just in time, too, since Dad arrives a few minutes early. You wonder if Jeff's noticed you've been using the ball pit. He probably doesn't care. He probably forgets it even exists.

"Dad," you say as he drives down Main Street, "was there ever another restaurant where Jeff's is now?" You're trying to be all cool about it; you can't imagine your dad would be particularly suspicious or anything of this question.

But he furrows his eyebrows and this expression passes across his face, like a cloud floating across the sun. "Uh, yeah, I guess," he says. Suddenly he seems super focused on the empty road.

"Yeah, someone mentioned something about a Freddy's arcade thing? From like way back in the '80s?"

Dad takes in a deep breath. Then he says, "Yeah."

"In 1985, you were probably close to my age. Did you ever go to the arcade there?" Why is Dad, who loves to talk so much, now suddenly super clammed up about everything?

"I liked arcades. I don't know if I went in 1985. It closed around then, I think. So yeah, I don't know. Let's talk about what we want for dinner."

The subject was officially changed but you feel strange now. Why is Dad being all weird about it? You're pretty sure the arcade wasn't closed in 1985 because you were just playing games there. Maybe he's talking about a different restaurant? You'll ask Chip and Mike about it tomorrow.

Of course, time being relative means it takes forever for tomorrow to come because you want it to so much, but it finally does and you are now back at Jeff's with your usual slice. He walks into the kitchen and you are back up on your feet, but you pause. You still feel weird about Dad's behavior yesterday. Maybe you shouldn't go into the pit this time? But you have questions for your new friends, and also it's just so nice to go to the arcade and have fun.

- **DAD MUST HAVE MADE A MISTAKE AND, ANYWAY, HE'S ALWAYS A BIT WEIRD. IF YOU GO BACK INTO THE PIT, TURN TO PAGE 43.**
- **DAD MIGHT BE WEIRD, BUT SOMETHING TELLS YOU MAYBE IT'S BEST TO AVOID THE PIT TODAY. IF YOU DECIDE AGAINST GOING INTO IT, TURN TO PAGE 11.**

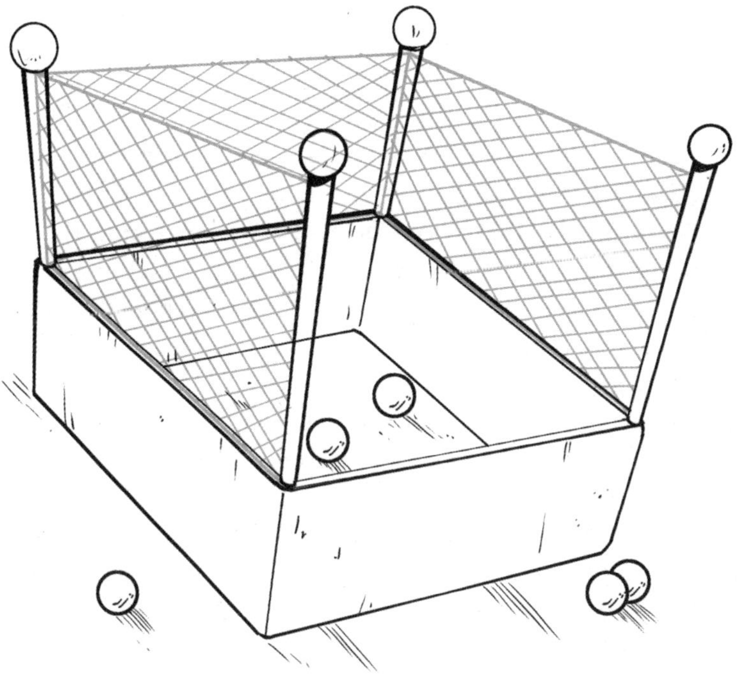

You all laugh at the bunny ears and you wonder if it's maybe time to ask them about the rabbit, but when you turn to look at it standing in its corner, something inside you tells you no. You quickly shove the ears in your backpack and get back to playing games.

The conversation turns to movies but you keep glancing over to the corner, looking at the rabbit.

"Seriously? You liked *The Eternal Song*? It was so boring," Mike is saying. You're not really paying attention.

"Oh come on, it's good! You just have crap taste. Right, Oz?" Chip says.

You hear your new nickname but it doesn't fully register until he asks you again.

"Oh, uh, yeah."

"Dude!" says Mike.

"What?"

Chip is laughing. "See, he agrees you have crap taste!"

Shoot, you hadn't actually heard the question. Now you feel bad.

"Well, what movies do you like, then?" asks Mike, scoring in air hockey. The lights flash and there's the sound of recorded cheering of a crowd.

You realize this is a complicated question. You could say you like those old monster movies, those are even older than the 1980s, but if you say that, they might think you're a huge nerd. But you can't say any movies from after 1985 and it's not like you keep track of exact movie dates. You decide to take a swing and hope you're right: "Uh, *E.T.*?"

"Dude, that's like from three years ago! You need to seriously get out more! Do they not have movie theaters where you're from?"

Sure they do, they also have Netflix and YouTube . . . but you can't tell them that.

"It's still a good movie," you say quietly. You're embarrassed and so used to being bullied for your tastes you can feel your cheeks turning red.

"Yeah, it totally is, but let's make a plan to see a new movie together so we can get you into the future!" says Chip with a smile.

You look at him. No mean comment? No making fun? Just quick teasing and then a plan to hang out more? You're not used to this. You wish you could actually go to a movie theater with these guys.

Well, maybe you can. You don't actually know if you're able to leave the arcade or not. There's a thought. Could you explore the whole 1985 version of your town? Could you go farther? Like, to a big city like New York or L.A.? Could you see what the whole world was like in 1985? And could you do it all and still be back at Jeff's in time for Dad to pick you up? The possibilities are kind of endless. Your mind is seriously blown. You could have adventures in the past and the present. Or, you suppose, Chip and Mike's future.

"Into the future?" you say with a bit of a smile. If only they knew . . .

"Okay, I'm scoping out the scene. I've got tokens on three games now, one of them has to be free, be right back!" says Chip.

"Yeah, I'll go grab drinks. Oz?" asks Mike.

"I'm good."

And you really are. Better than good. For the first time in a long time, you feel that you actually belong. You lean against the air hockey table and look over at the rabbit. It's still staring at you. You're feeling pretty awesome now, pretty up for anything. Suddenly it raises a hand and crooks its finger at you in that "come here" kind of motion. You look over your shoulder. Is it signaling you? Looks like it. Super weird.

- **YOU DON'T HAVE TIME TO DEAL WITH WEIRD RABBITS. IF YOU SHAKE YOUR HEAD AND TURN BACK TO THE TABLE, WAITING FOR THE GUYS TO COME BACK, TURN TO PAGE 38.**
- **YOU'RE FULL OF CONFIDENCE AND THINK, "WHAT THE HECK." IF YOU CHECK OUT WHAT THIS RABBIT WANTS, TURN TO PAGE 107.**

You head over to the door and it opens easily. And yup, sure enough, there's a back hallway here. You walk down the bland gray hall looking for that "Stop." It's funny staring at the 8-bit Freddy posters on the wall. They're kind of cool-looking. You kind of want one for yourself to put up in your room. If you ever get back to your time, of course. If you ever get out of 8-bit world.

You come across another door, so you open it and step inside. You find yourself in a storage room with tall shelves stacked with old toys, some Freddy action figures and plush yellow chicks wearing LET'S EAT bibs. There's a mop and bucket in the corner.

And that's when you see four little 8-bit kids sitting on chairs wearing party hats.

"Help!" one calls out to you, though you don't actually hear him say it. Instead, the words appear in a black text box above his head, spelled out in pixels.

Help?

You realize they are actually tied to the chairs.

"Please save us!" another calls out. Again, a text box appears over her head. White letters on a black background.

You don't know what to do. All you want is to escape this game, but it looks like you might need to play it to get out. And it has something to do with these kids. You just want to find an exit, not waste time like this! Then again, maybe helping the kids will help you find the way out?

- **EVEN IF IT DOESN'T HELP YOU ESCAPE IN THE END, IT'S STILL THE RIGHT THING TO DO. IF YOU DECIDE TO UNTIE THEM, TURN TO PAGE 49.**
- **NO, YOU DON'T HAVE TIME TO PLAY THE ACTUAL GAME. IF YOU TURN AROUND TO LEAVE, TURN TO PAGE 50.**

You are expecting all the sounds you've grown used to when you emerge into 1985—what you are not expecting is noise. Not just any noise, but chaotic panicked horrifying noise, like a high-pitched alarm going off right by your ear, blinding you with a pain that's both physical but also something deeply, profoundly in your gut. The screams hit you first. Bloodcurdling and like something out of a horror movie. The sound comes from all directions as your eyes focus on the chaos in front of you. No one is playing games. No one is eating food. Everyone is running around, calling out names, frantic in their searching for something, or someone. There's a crowd building at the exit, and everyone is trying to get out but making it impossible by pushing and shoving at one another. A small child is a sobbing snotty mess next to you in the ball pit. Just sitting there screaming his little lungs out. He's scooped up by his mom who doesn't even seem to notice you.

Where are Chip and Mike? And what is going on?

You step out of the pit, stunned. Everyone around you is moving so quickly it's like you are walking in slow motion. Everything is a whirl of sound and movement.

Everything except one thing.

One person.

One . . . thing?

The person in the yellow rabbit mascot costume is standing in the corner like always. Perfectly still. The only stillness in the whole room. Even the animatronic band is still playing their happy little song, which, with the hysteria and screaming in the room, just amps up their creep factor by a thousand.

But not the yellow rabbit. It stands. It stares.

Then it motions to you. Like it did yesterday.

- MAYBE HE KNOWS WHAT'S GOING ON. MAYBE ALL THIS TIME HE'S HAD THE ANSWERS YOU'VE BEEN LOOKING FOR. IF YOU FOLLOW HIM, TURN TO PAGE 45.
- NO, THIS IS CRAZY. YOU WILL *NOT* ENTER THIS NIGHTMARE. THIS ISN'T YOUR TIME TO GO, AND NOW YOU'RE THINKING THAT MAYBE THIS PLACE DID SHUT DOWN IN 1985 AFTER ALL. THAT MAYBE DAD'S WEIRD REACTION MAKES A LOT OF SENSE NOW IF SOMETHING HORRIFYING THAT CAUSED ALL THIS CHAOS HAPPENED THEN. IF YOU DON'T FOLLOW HIM, TURN TO PAGE 30.

You walk carefully across to the rabbit, partially in order to avoid the manic, panicked people tearing about the place like chickens with their heads cut off, and also partially because you have this weird feeling, this pull in your gut, like you are drawn to the rabbit. Like it's more than just curiosity. It's a need. A need to understand. And somehow the rabbit has the answers. It's *always* had the answers.

Up close, the fur of the costume is even more matted and ratty than from afar. A stale smell wafts over to you, not just of years and years of body odor collecting in the fabric but something more sinister. Something otherworldly. No. No, that's ridiculous. It's just the smell of an unwashed mascot costume. And yet . . .

The rabbit's eyes are cold and dead, and yet somehow, they stare at you. You try to see the man in the suit, you look into the dark void of the rabbit's open mouth, but you are greeted with simply pitch-blackness. The rabbit is the person. The person is the rabbit. You should leave. You should really go back into the pit. But as the rabbit turns to lead you through the back door, you follow it.

You have a choice.

Or do you?

You follow it down a hallway, one of those industrial spaces that are so glaringly opposite of the fun and careful design of the public space. Just a hall of gray. Walls. Ceiling. Floors. There is the odd poster on the wall. Some with public health and safety in mind. Some with Freddy's band on them advertising special birthday parties.

You find the public health and safety ones way more enticing somehow.

You come to another gray door.

The rabbit opens it, then stands back.

It wants you to go first.

That feels wrong somehow and yet . . .

You go first.

Your eyes adjust to the darkness. You're in a storage room. What's so interesting about that?

You don't see the kids, initially. The first thing you see is the party hats. You see their colorful pointy shapes, in all the darkness and in all the gray, and they draw you farther into the room. A few more steps in and that's when you see them. The kids wearing the hats. Sitting there, on the floor, propped up.

Lifeless.

Like dolls.

Except they aren't dolls. They are human kids.

And they are all dead.

The horror washes over you, making you lightheaded and dizzy. You want to throw up. You want to scream.

You need to run.

- **IF YOU CHARGE PAST THE RABBIT OUT OF THE ROOM AND SEE AN EXIT DOOR TO YOUR RIGHT, TURN TO PAGE 109.**
- **IF YOU CHARGE PAST THE RABBIT, OUT OF THE ROOM, AND BACK INTO THE RESTAURANT TO GET BACK TO THE BALL PIT AS FAST AS POSSIBLE, TURN TO PAGE 48.**
- **IF YOU CHARGE PAST THE RABBIT OUT OF THE ROOM AND THEN SLOW DOWN WHEN YOU ARE BACK IN THE RESTAURANT, TURN TO PAGE 47.**

You are careful not to draw attention to yourself as you reenter the restaurant. It's not too hard, since everyone is still running around screaming. You hear the names being called out again and then you wonder, *Are those the names of the kids you just saw? Of the dead kids sitting on the floor in the storage closet?* You should tell someone, anyone. Call the cops. Talk to an adult. Where are Chip and Mike? They'd listen to you, they'd trust you.

You have made it to the pit and dare to look over your shoulder to see if the rabbit has followed you. It hasn't. It isn't anywhere to be seen. You quickly climb into the ball pit.

➤ TURN TO PAGE 60.

You rush through the chaos and realize you are now running around and freaking out just like every other patron. *How fun it is to fit in.* Not now, sarcastic brain! You glance over your shoulder, but the rabbit isn't coming after you. You aren't about to take any chances and actually speed up. You are full-on sprinting toward the ball pit as if you are determined to get first prize in a race. You make it and dive into it like it's a pool, just headfirst, even though you have no idea how deep it's going to be this time. Your hand grabs something small and solid as you reach downward, pulling yourself into the pit. It's hard to see in the dark swirling colors, but you know you're supposed to look at it. Even in the panic and fear, something about this thing in your hand matters. You look at it closely—it's half of a Freddy token. But this one is gold. You haven't seen one of these before. There's something in your memory that tells you you've heard of a gold token before but can't remember. This is ridiculous . . . why are you worried about a stupid half piece of plastic? None of this is important right now! You need to get back to your time! You put the half in your pocket (if you started the game with half a Freddy token, you now have a whole Freddy token). You start your count to a hundred.

➤ **TURN TO PAGE 60.**

You work your way down the row of kids, untying their hands and their feet from the chairs. It's really weird seeing your own 8-bit hands as you do it. But you try not to focus on that. You finish and stand upright waiting for the kids to get up or something.

But they don't move.

You walk around them one more time, just to double-check you've untied everything. You can't see anything that might be holding them down.

What are you supposed to do, exactly?

"What am I supposed to do?" you say. Or at least you *try* to say it. Your words come out as jumbled sounds, almost more like notes on an instrument than words. Why don't you at least get a text box, too? Seems unfair.

Well, this is frustrating.

You hear a *bang* from down the hall and spin on your heel to look at the open door.

Next, you hear heavy footsteps heading your way.

You turn again and see a giant box of party supplies in the corner.

➤ **IF YOU JUMP BEHIND THE PARTY SUPPLIES TO HIDE, TURN TO PAGE 53.**

➤ **IF YOU STAND THERE FACING THE DOOR AND WAITING TO SEE WHO IS COMING, TURN TO PAGE 58.**

There's no time to help the pixel kids. You need to get out of this game! You don't belong here! You head back out into the hall. And right into a giant 8-bit yellow rabbit. Or . . . no. Not an actual rabbit. It's hard to tell because it's a pile of giant pixels, but somehow you understand that this isn't just some big bunny like in a cartoon, but someone wearing a mascot costume. You don't know why, but that horrifies you more than if it had been a cartoon bunny. Even though a giant bunny in real life is way weirder than just some person wearing a costume.

There's something ominous about this rabbit, though. Something not quite right.

As you try to figure out what's weird about it, the rabbit opens its mouth wide. Wider than any mouth should open. You stare inside its gaping maw and see sharp teeth, or what you assume are sharp teeth—nothing can really be sharp-looking when it's all made of tiny squares. Huh. Weird.

You really should be more scared you realize when the rabbit lunges at you and pierces your flesh with the teeth that don't seem sharp. You cry out, but the sound is more like a series of notes than a scream.

Everything fades to blackness.

A perpetual night.

Forever dead.

Until you regenerate back in front of the arcade game. You are a little dizzy and confused. It takes you a moment to realize what's happened.

Oh. I can't die. Or maybe you only have a certain number of lives? *But it's a game. I'm in a game*, you tell yourself.

The pain was real, though. You wince when remembering it. You're not sure how many times you want to be torn to shreds by a rabbit mascot.

Well, you're back at the start now. And you still need to

escape from this game. You really don't have much of a choice, so you might as well try again!

➤ TURN TO PAGE 31.

You dive back into the pit and away from Dad. You feel a little guilty and almost immediately decide you're going to turn back around and face the music. You shouldn't just ignore him like that, he doesn't deserve it. Just as you are about to turn around, you suddenly find yourself face-to-face with the giant yellow rabbit mascot! You have no idea what it's doing there and you are stunned, too shocked to move or say anything.

It reaches out for you and grabs you hard, pulling you down farther into the pit. Deeper and deeper, it draws you in close. And then, though it's hard to see, it opens its mouth wide revealing rows of razor-sharp teeth. You struggle and cry out: "Dad!"

But it's too late.

The rabbit bites down hard.

GAME OVER

>TO TRY AGAIN TURN TO PAGE 2

You peer out from behind the box to see a giant yellow 8-bit rabbit enter the room. Even though it's made of pixels and it's hard to see details, somehow you get the impression that the game isn't telling you this is an actual giant rabbit. You think for some reason this is a person inside a rabbit costume. You don't know why you are supposed to know that, or what difference it makes, but you feel very uncomfortable by the thought. A little scared, even.

Oh, maybe that's why you were meant to think it. The game *wants* you to feel scared.

You realize then that the rabbit is carrying another kid in over its shoulder. You watch as the rabbit places the kid on another chair. The kid tries to run away, but the rabbit catches him as he rises from the chair and pushes him back down on it—hard. The rabbit quickly places a party hat on the kid's head and suddenly the kid sits perfectly still. The rabbit then ties the kid to the chair like the other kids had been tied up and then leaves.

You feel adrenaline pumping through your veins. You understand what you have to do now!

You wait a beat longer to make sure the rabbit isn't on its way back anytime soon, and when you feel like enough time has passed you quietly sneak out from your hiding spot and move over to the kids. You untie the new kid. Then as quickly as you can, you remove all the party hats from the kids' heads. The moment you do, the kids are instantly up on their feet. They can move around freely now!

"Thank you!" appears above a girl's head.

"We need to escape quickly!" appears over the boy to her left.

Okay, okay, that's the next task. You might as well treat this like an actual video game. A video game where you can get injured and bleed pixels, but still.

Time to escape the back room!

- IF YOU LOOK AROUND THE ROOM AND NOTICE A LADDER IN THE CORNER THAT SEEMS TO ACCESS A VENT IN THE CEILING, TURN TO PAGE 62.
- IF YOU DECIDE TO CAREFULLY PEER AROUND THE CORNER TO SEE IF THE COAST IS CLEAR, TURN TO PAGE 65.

You stand up in the pit as Dad marches over.

"What were you thinking, hiding in that nasty old thing?" he says. "Didn't you hear me calling you?"

"Sorry, I was distracted," you say as you climb out. "Distracted" is putting it mildly.

Dad does not seem impressed by that excuse. He shakes his head at you. "Pretty sure you were ignoring me. You haven't been very nice to me lately, and I don't think I deserved this. You really had me worried."

You lower your eyes. You don't want to admit he's right, but also he has no idea what you've just been through in 1985 and you don't think you can control your emotions enough right now not to cry.

Dad leans over the ball pit, examining it more closely. "Look at how dirty this is. Your mother—"

Suddenly a pair of yellow arms launches through the balls and grabs Dad around his torso. You cry out and leap back as Dad is pulled into the pit and is completely submerged. There is chaos under the balls, and you see your dad kick out his leg, but then it falls back under. You finally snap out of your shock and quickly dive into the pit, pulling balls out of the way while trying to dig for him. Has he been pulled into the past?

"Dad!" you cry out. "Dad, are you okay?"

A pair of ratty large yellow ears emerges from the pit. Followed by those eyes, dead and soulless. Those eyes you know way too well now. The rabbit mascot stares at you, the rest of its face and body still submerged. You stare back. Fear has got you in its grasp. It feels both cold and hot, and now you've forgotten how to breathe. You stumble back and grab on to the edge of the pit.

The rabbit rises slowly, standing tall and looming over you. It stares out into the restaurant. And then, with a sharp, sudden movement, it is staring down at you.

You scramble backward, pulling yourself over the edge of the pit and falling onto the floor, your legs kicking out from under you as you try to get yourself to standing. The rabbit walks toward you, stepping out of the pit easily, and still it comes for you.

You want to scream, you need to. At least yell for help!

But you can't, as you are now paralyzed with fear. You stop trying to stand. You just stare.

The rabbit continues to loom over you.

Then it extends its hand. As if to help you up.

You can't take it. You certainly don't *want* to take it.

But you feel that familiar pull at your middle. And for some reason, you take its hand.

You are brought to standing. You now stare at each other and finally you have the ability to speak, "What did you do to my dad?"

The yellow hand clamps hard around your wrist, and the rabbit turns and pulls you along behind him. You try to break free, but its grasp is too tight.

Jeff emerges from the kitchen as you pass by the counter.

"See you later, guys!" he says in his classic monotone. Does he not see the giant yellow rabbit kidnapping you? "Next time I'll get you a slice to go."

You turn to look at the ball pit, hoping Dad has pulled himself out, but he's still in there, somewhere. How can you just leave him behind? Well, it's not like you have much of a choice.

You are dragged out of Jeff's and into the daylight.

You flinch at how bright it is. The rabbit does, too, releasing its grip slightly on your wrist. It hasn't totally let you go, but maybe you can wiggle your hand through and escape?

- NO, YOU CAN'T. YOU HAVE NO IDEA WHAT'S GOING ON AND YOU'RE SCARED ANY REACTION WILL ONLY MAKE THE RABBIT ANGRY. IF YOU LET IT LEAD YOU TO YOUR DAD'S CAR, TURN TO PAGE 61.
- THIS IS YOUR CHANCE! IF YOU BREAK FREE FROM THE RABBIT'S GRIP AND RUN AS FAST AS YOU CAN DOWN THE STREET, TURN TO PAGE 69.

You wait as the footsteps grow louder and louder. With each step you get more nervous and a feeling of dread washes over you. You think maybe you should have hidden yourself instead, but it's too late. In walks a giant 8-bit yellow rabbit. Or . . . no. Not an actual rabbit. It's hard to tell because it's a pile of giant pixels, but somehow you understand that this isn't just some big bunny, like in a cartoon, but someone wearing a mascot costume. You don't know why but that horrifies you more than if it had been a cartoon bunny. Even though a giant bunny in real life is way weirder than just some person wearing a costume.

There's something ominous about this rabbit, though. Something not quite right.

You suddenly get the strongest feeling that you need to run. Now! You dash away from the beast around behind the kids, and it drops the kid it is carrying over its shoulder. You only notice this new kid when it lands on the ground. The kid jumps up to standing and tries to rush away, past the rabbit, but the giant mascot produces a birthday hat and puts it on the kid's head. The kid slumps to the ground as if stunned. What on earth? The rabbit pulls another hat out of somewhere and starts walking toward you. No no no. You absolutely will *not* let it put that hat on your head!

You dart out to the side and dive for the exit. There's almost enough space, but the rabbit manages to grab you by your shirt and drag you into the room. It slams the hat on your head and you feel suddenly very calm and sleepy.

Very at peace.

Oh, you realize then, *maybe this is all just a dream*. Yes. Of course. That is the only thing that makes any sense. You are asleep at home in your bed. Your parents are in the room next door. Jinx the cat is curled up in the corner. You are safe.

It's all just a dream.

Oh thank goodness.

You smile at the rabbit.

The rabbit stares down at you and then opens its mouth wide. Wider than any mouth should open. You stare inside its gaping maw and see sharp teeth, or what you assume are sharp teeth—nothing can really be sharp-looking when it's all made of tiny squares. Huh. Funny.

You really should be more scared when the rabbit lunges at you and pierces your flesh with dull-looking teeth. You cry out, but the sound is more like a series of notes than a scream.

Everything fades to blackness.

A perpetual night.

Forever dead.

Until you regenerate back in front of the arcade game. You are a little dizzy and confused. It takes you a moment to understand what's happened.

Oh. I can't die. Or maybe you only have a certain number of lives? But it's a game. *I'm in a game*, you tell yourself.

The pain was real, though. You wince when remembering it. You're not sure how many times you want to be torn to shreds by a rabbit mascot.

Well, you're back at the start now. And you still need to escape from this game. You really don't have much of a choice, so you might as well try again!

➤ **TURN BACK TO PAGE 31.**

You finally emerge back in your time, in the dusty ball pit at Jeff's. Oh, how blissful it is to not hear screaming, to smell the dank aroma, to feel the heavy weight of grease in the air. You're home. In your stupid boring time. Maybe boring isn't such a bad thing. It's better than dead kids and chaos, that's for sure.

Your wave of relief is quickly replaced by a heated feeling of panic when you notice your dad walking around the restaurant booths, looking for you. Shoot, he's early.

Dad spots you and marches over.

"Oswald, what are you doing?"

"I was just . . . in the ball pit." Which is pretty much the most obvious thing ever to say.

Dad looks seriously annoyed. "I've been looking for you, calling your name and everything, and you've been hiding in a dirty old ball pit? Why would you waste my time like that?"

- **NO, YOU DON'T NEED THIS. MAYBE IF YOU GO BACK INTO THE PIT YOU'LL COME OUT ON A DIFFERENT DAY WHEN YOU CAN JUST PLAY GAMES AGAIN WITH YOUR FRIENDS. IF YOU GO BACK INTO THE PIT, TURN TO PAGE 52.**
- **IF YOU FEEL BAD AND CLIMB OUT OF THE BALL PIT TO FACE YOUR DAD'S ANGER, TURN TO PAGE 55.**

You climb into the passenger seat like always, and the car takes off faster than Dad ever normally drives. Your heart is in your throat and the fear is overwhelming, like it's wrapping itself around you, holding you tight. But this doesn't feel like a hug—it's more like a boa constrictor slowly squeezing you to death. You glance to your left. You don't want to make eye contact or stare, and you certainly don't want to make it obvious you are looking. The rabbit is staring out the front windshield. Those empty eyes seemingly observing the empty street. Where is it taking you? Why is this happening? Is Dad still alive?

The boa constrictor squeezes tighter.

Please let Dad be alive. Please. Please don't let the last conversation you guys ever have be some stupid angry one. You're so over stupid angry conversations. You feel so guilty.

The rabbit stops at the one traffic light. That stupid pointless light. Obviously no cars are coming from any direction. And yet this freaky rabbit costume guy obeys the rules of the road even when it's pointless?

Why is that something you're thinking about? You should jump out of the car now while you have a chance! You need to escape! To get some help! Or save Dad! Yet why does it feel pointless, like even if you tried, the rabbit would catch you?

- **NOW IS NOT THE TIME TO GIVE UP! IF YOU DECIDE TO JUMP OUT OF THE CAR, TURN TO PAGE 64.**
- **YOU FEEL THIS HEAVY HOPELESSNESS MIXED WITH WEIGHTED FEAR. IF YOU STAY IN THE CAR, TURN TO PAGE 63.**

You gesture to the kids to follow you and cross the room to the ladder. It's really hard to tell how secure it is since it's made of pixels, but you figure it wouldn't exist in this game if you weren't meant to climb it.

You go up the ladder first, carefully, until you reach the large round vent at the top of the wall. You glance into it. It's definitely big enough for a person to fit. And since most vents in real life aren't, you take it as another sign that you should use it. Otherwise, why would the game have a human-sized vent to crawl through?

You pull yourself into the vent and then turn around so your head is poking out.

You try to speak but of course it comes out as all notes, so you shake your head and gesture for the kids to follow you. You remember your parents always told you to do the right thing.

Thankfully they understand. You move deeper into the vent as, one by one, each kid climbs inside. Once everyone is in, you turn and lead them into the ventilation system, crawling along as quietly as you can.

You reach a T-section.

You can go right or left here. You look back at the kids to see if they have a preference, but they just stare back at you. It would seem you're the one in charge of all the decisions in this game.

➤ IF YOU GO RIGHT, TURN TO PAGE 159.

➤ YOU GO LEFT, TURN TO PAGE 157.

➤ IF YOU HAVE A MAP OF THE PIZZERIA, TURN TO PAGE 162.

The light finally turns green. And you continue on your journey. You realize as you go that the rabbit is taking the same route Dad always does to get home. Wait, is it taking you back to your house? Why? And how does the rabbit know the way home? Just another question to add to the pile in your brain as he takes every correct turn and pulls up in front of your house. You thought for sure this was a classic kidnapping scenario, but does a kidnapper usually take a kid right to their own front door? To be fair, you have limited experience with kidnapping, and definitely zero experience with yellow rabbit mascots who attack dads and drag you across town with them.

You are led inside your own home and your cat, Jinx, wanders up in that way she always does, like she doesn't care that you finally came home, she just happened to be passing by the front door the second you showed up. But instead of flopping onto her side for scratches, her tail turns pine-cone poofy and she hisses at the rabbit, running away like you probably should have in the car.

In a way it makes you feel a bit more sane. This whole situation *is* seriously freaky. It also makes you feel determined again to get out of it.

"I'm just gonna . . . go to my room . . ." you explain to the rabbit who just stares back at you. But it lets you go and you dart up the stairs into your room as fast as you can, closing the door behind you.

You're alone and safe. For now. Time to set a plan, any plan, into motion!

YOU NEED TO GET AWAY FROM THE RABBIT AS FAST AS POSSIBLE! IF YOU GO TO YOUR WINDOW AND OPEN IT TO ESCAPE, TURN TO PAGE 75.

IF YOU SEND YOUR MOM A TEXT THAT IT'S AN EMERGENCY AND SHE HAS TO COME HOME RIGHT NOW, TURN TO PAGE 66.

You can't outrun a car.

The car plows over you.

GAME OVER

>TO TRY AGAIN TURN TO PAGE 2

You peer around the corner and look both up and down the hall. The coast is clear, no rabbit in sight. Your plan was to go back into the restaurant and out the front entrance to escape, but now you notice there is also a back exit to your right. Maybe it would be safer to go that way? So that you don't risk any potential rabbit run-ins . . .

- NO, IT'S BETTER TO STICK WITH THE ORIGINAL PLAN, NO NEED TO MAKE THINGS MORE COMPLICATED. IF YOU CHOOSE TO STICK WITH THE RESTAURANT ESCAPE ROUTE, TURN TO PAGE 76.
- AN EXIT IS AN EXIT, AND YOU WANT TO GET THESE KIDS OUT OF HERE AS FAST AS POSSIBLE! IF YOU CHOOSE THE BACK EXIT, TURN TO PAGE 167.

Mom comes home fifteen minutes later. You hear her open the front door and slam it shut. Okay, so maybe she isn't quite as calm as you'd thought she'd be, you're usually the only door slammer in the family. You wait in your room for her to appear, but it seems to take her forever. For a second you worry the rabbit has gotten her, too, and you feel like such an idiot not warning her about it in the text. But finally after what feels like forever, she opens the door.

"Oswald, what's wrong?" Her eyes are wide and she looks almost like she's going to cry. Oh, that's not good, you definitely don't want to make her cry. But you also have to tell her the truth. She needs to know. As awful as it is.

"It's Dad . . . he's . . ." How exactly do you explain it? The fear and panic you've been holding deep inside you is welling up, overwhelming you. It's hard to explain.

"What about Dad?"

"He's gone," you finally eke out.

"What do you mean 'gone'?" She reaches up and pushes your hair back from your forehead, and you realize just then that you're a sweaty mess.

"He's . . . at Jeff's . . ." You can't explain it. But you have to.

"Honey, are you okay? Dad's here, I just saw him. He's taking a nap in our room."

You don't fully understand what she's said. It doesn't make sense. Dad is definitely not home. He's deep beneath the surface of a ball pit, maybe in the past, maybe dead. You know this for a fact.

Or do you? You think hard to yourself. When would he have come home? You would have heard the front door like when Mom came home. But also . . . why would she lie? Maybe you've been so distracted you missed it?

Maybe . . . now here was a thought . . . maybe the rabbit thing wasn't real? Maybe it was Dad all along, just like Jeff implied? Maybe you are going crazy and just seeing rabbits everywhere?

Not that that would be a good thing, but it would be better than something bad having happened to Dad.

"He's okay?" you ask. "He's home?"

Mom nods. She looks worried and now holds the back of her hand to your forehead. Does she think you're sick and have a fever? You're not sick, you're just . . . maybe actually . . . You think about 1985. You remember the screams. You remember the dead kids. It feels all like a horrible nightmare, and maybe, well, maybe that's what it was. Maybe you fell asleep in the pit somehow, or maybe you're just imagining things. Maybe you actually do have some kind of fever.

"How about you get some rest? School starts tomorrow and I think you might have been overexerting yourself a bit today."

School. Yes, school does start tomorrow. How did the summer pass so quickly? Well, 1985 helped. But was it real? Had any of it happened? You feel very tired suddenly. And even though you haven't had dinner yet, you really just want to go to bed. You nod.

"Yeah, okay, that's a good idea." Mom smiles at you. "And Dad's really just napping, in the other room?"

"Dad's really just napping."

This weight lifts off your chest and even though you don't quite feel happy, the relief is enough to make you super sleepy.

Mom leaves and you go to bed. You sleep through dinner and all the way to your alarm going off for school the next morning. You wake up feeling refreshed, feeling hopeful. 1985 seems like all just a bad dream. Plus, you are starving and you can smell breakfast floating up from the kitchen.

You practically skip downstairs and see Mom standing over some eggs and bacon frying on the stove. Nothing has ever looked so tasty in your life!

"Morning!" you say.

"Morning!" she replies. "You look very well rested!"

"I am." You turn with a grin to the table to find your seat, and there, in Dad's spot, holding Dad's paper, with Dad's mug of coffee sitting beside him, is the yellow rabbit. Just sitting there.

You feel dizzy. You have to hold on to the top of your chair to steady yourself.

"Where's Dad?" you ask. Fear grips at your throat and you barely manage to get the words out.

"What do you mean, silly? He's right there," says Mom, pointing at the rabbit with her spatula. She shakes her head and turns back to the bacon. "Honestly, Oswald, this is getting a little much. I don't understand the missing Dad game, but it's time for some breakfast and to get ready for school."

- **YOU DON'T KNOW WHAT TO DO. YOU ONLY KNOW DEEP IN YOUR GUT YOU HAVE TO PLAY ALONG. IF YOU PRETEND THE RABBIT IS DAD, TURN TO PAGE 70.**
- **THIS ISN'T A GAME! SHE HAS TO UNDERSTAND! IF YOU EXPLAIN TO HER WHAT HAPPENED AND THAT THE RABBIT IS SITTING RIGHT THERE, TURN TO PAGE 74.**

You run as fast as you can away from the rabbit down the street, skidding as you quickly take the next corner. You're not exactly sure where you are running. Home? Maybe you can make it to Mom's work in time? Or the police? You're in panic mode and know you need to get as much space between you and that thing as you can.

There is a loud screech of tire on asphalt, and you look over your shoulder to see Dad's car following you fast. The rabbit is in the driver's seat! Crap! You run faster as the car chases you through town. The place is so empty there are basically no witnesses, or at least no one seems interested in helping a kid being mowed down by a maniacal rabbit driving a car!

You keep running and running, but you are getting tired, and there's no way you are faster than a car!

➤ GO TO PAGE 64.

You manage to swallow a few bites of breakfast sitting opposite the rabbit. It doesn't do anything and just sits there reading the paper. Mom chats happily with it, though, explaining her plan for the day and talking about how exciting it is that "their" son is going into sixth grade. Of course the rabbit doesn't respond, but she reacts as if it does. She even laughs as if it has told a hilarious joke.

What the heck?

You finish breakfast and go upstairs to get ready for school. You tell yourself that at least it's a way to get out of this house and away from the crazy rabbit. But how can you just go about a regular first day back to school with everything that's happening to you? And why can't you just run away? Go to the police, maybe? Or even just a neighbor? Anyone could help. But then again, you tell yourself, if Mom sees the rabbit as Dad and Jeff sees the rabbit as Dad, well, maybe all adults do? Maybe only kids and cats can see the truth.

The rabbit drives you to school, and you feel so alone and lost. Why is it doing this? What is its plan? If it wants to kill you, then it should just kill you! Why does it want to be Dad, of all people? Boring, cheap, tries too hard, loves stupid movies and terrible country music, just wants you to have an okay summer, Dad. Man, you miss him. And man, you feel guilty for getting so mad at him this summer. You'd be so happy to have an argument with him right now and not be sitting in strange silence next to this decaying rabbit mascot. The fur looks even more matted and stained than yesterday if that's possible.

It drops you off at school and you wonder if any of the other kids can see the mascot in the car, but no one is paying attention. They're all excited to be back and hugging one another and catching up from the summer. You have no one to catch up with, so you walk to class alone.

You sit at the desk second from the back on the right side. The same location you sit at in every classroom for every class every year. But there's no Ben on your left to talk to. You instinctively pull out your notebook but you realize you can't even draw or doodle anymore. Those animal band characters are now real, even if they're not like *real* real, you saw them, you time-traveled, kids watched them play their little animatronic song.

Five dead kids in a storage room.

Heads lolling to the side, empty dead eyes.

You shove the notebook back in your bag and try to listen to the lesson instead. It's nothing you don't already know about integers. But it's better than thinking about the past.

Or home.

At lunch, you wander over to the old swing set at the far end of the schoolyard. No one ever hangs out there, the grass is all overgrown, and the grounds crew seem to have forgotten it exists. But now someone is sitting on one of the swings. A girl you've never seen before.

"Uh, hi," you say. You're not sure if you should sit or not.

The girl looks up at you and smiles. "Hi! I'm Gabrielle. I'm new."

"I'm Oswald." You don't know what else to say.

"It's nice to meet you!" She seems happy about that even though she's all the way over here on her own as if she's trying to avoid people. "It's weird these are the only swings, huh?"

"Yeah, they came and tore down the old jungle gym two years ago for safety reasons," you say. "Now it's just the slide and that climbing rock thing."

You both look back toward the school where everyone else is hanging out and playing.

"Well, it's okay, I like to read during lunch anyway," she says. You notice the book in her lap.

"Oh, sorry, I'll leave you alone." You feel instantly guilty for bugging her.

"No, it's nice to have company and to make a new friend! Sit!"

She really seems to mean it, so you sit on the other swing next to her.

Say something, Oswald, you tell yourself. *Be friendly.* "Uh, what's the book about?"

Gabrielle beams at the question and holds the book up so you can see the cover. "Gods and Monsters" is written across it in big bold letters, and there's a picture of a giant monster with many heads on long snakelike necks looming over a small figure in the foreground. The figure is holding up his sword to battle it. "It's about Greek myths! It's so cool." She points to the picture on the cover. "This is the Hercules myth that I just finished reading, about him fighting the Hydra. And now I've started reading about Theseus!"

Her excitement is infectious, and for the first time since you saw the rabbit at the kitchen table, you feel a little happy. You want to know more!

➤ IF YOU ASK HER TO TELL YOU ABOUT THESEUS, TURN TO PAGE 124.

➤ IF YOU ASK HER TO TELL YOU ABOUT HERCULES AND THE HYDRA, TURN TO PAGE 77.

You stay as still as you possibly can. You don't even breathe. You just stare and watch as the rabbit stands there beneath you. What is it doing? Why is it just standing there? Can it still hear you with those giant ears? No, that's stupid, the ears aren't real, he's a mascot. Can he smell you? Well, that seems even stupider.

You feel like you're going to pass out, but the rabbit finally walks off behind you. You wait a moment and then take in a deep breath.

Suddenly there is a crash from behind, and you turn to see large yellow arms reaching up through the bottom of the vent, grabbing and twisting, pulling on the torso of the kid behind you. The thrashing causes the vent to buckle, and you hold on to the metal with the tips of your fingers. Oh, there is no way this is going well for you.

The entire vent shaft collapses off the ceiling and you fall hard into the hallway. You, the kids, and the rabbit. The rabbit grabs at you as you fall, pulling you close, and somehow twists and breaks your neck.

Blackness.

Death.

Forever.

Until you regenerate back in front of the arcade game. You are a little dizzy and confused. It takes you a moment to understand what's happened.

Oh. I can't die. Or maybe you only have a certain number of lives? But it's a game. *I'm in a game*, you tell yourself.

The pain was real, though. You wince when remembering it. You're not sure how many times you want to be pulverized by a rabbit mascot.

Well, you're back at the start now. And you still need to escape from this game. You really don't have much of a choice, so you might as well try again!

➤ TURN TO PAGE 31.

"I know this isn't a game!" you shout. You need her to understand! You point at the rabbit. "That's not Dad. That's a giant yellow rabbit, and it hurt Dad! It did something bad to him! He's trapped in the ball pit at Jeff's Pizza!"

Mom is staring at you like you are crazy. And maybe you are. Maybe the stuff in the pit didn't happen, maybe 1985 didn't happen, but all you know is right now it feels super real and all you can do is deal with the situation in the moment. You know you sound crazy, but that is also part of the current situation you need to deal with!

"Sit down, now," your mom orders.

The rabbit stands ominously. It stares at you.

It raises its hand and points at you.

You don't know what he means, but you know it's a threat!

"No!" You pick up the thing closest to you, which happens to be a pancake from the stack, and throw it at the rabbit. The rabbit takes a step back and sits down hard on its chair.

"Oswald!"

You grab another pancake and another! The rabbit is distracted and seems almost as confused as you are. You run out of pancakes and so take advantage of his moment of confusion and run like heck out of the kitchen, down the hall, and out of the house.

You stand on the lawn panting, freaking out. . . . Now what?

➤ **IF YOU DECIDE TO RUN NEXT DOOR FOR HELP, TURN TO PAGE 116.**

➤ **IF YOU DECIDE TO GO TO JEFF'S, TURN TO PAGE 119.**

You cross your bedroom and carefully open your window. You look down. Man, two stories somehow looks way taller from up here than it does from the ground. Are you really about to do this? Escape from your house by going out the window? You've seen enough movies to know people do it all the time. Or maybe that's just a lie to make a story sound more interesting. Well, what other choice do you have? It's this or . . . what? Try to escape through the door with the rabbit in the house? Nah, that's not a good idea.

You examine the drop below you. There's a wooden trellis that runs under your window and to the ground and that could probably work as a kind of ladder. Yes, it's worth the risk. You have officially made up your mind, no turning back now! You're going to sneak out and go to Jeff's and save Dad! There's no time to waste!

You carefully climb through the window and hold on to the sill as you lower yourself down enough so that your toe hits the first hole in the trellis. It feels secure enough, so you do the same with your other foot. That feels secure as well. Okay, okay, this actually might just work. Maybe movies sometimes contain good ideas?

Now you just have to let go of the windowsill . . .

Crack!

The trellis was not built to handle your full weight! It snaps beneath you and you slip, falling to the ground and breaking your neck.

GAME OVER

>TO TRY AGAIN TURN TO PAGE 2

You try to tell the kids to follow you, but you only produce musical sounds. Not being able to talk in this game is a deeply frustrating experience.

You gesture at the kids with your hand and that seems to do the trick. You lead them as quickly and as quietly as you can down the hall. You reach the door back into the restaurant. You carefully open it and peek your head around the door to take stock of the room. That's when you notice the rabbit on the opposite side, near the birthday table.

Something appears in your peripheral vision and you look up. A text box with "Oh no!" has materialized above the kid standing next to you. *Oh no* indeed.

You can see the exit out of the restaurant into the street to the right. It's not that far away. And the rabbit's back is to you. Maybe you can sneak all the kids out of the restaurant if you just do it quietly and carefully? Or . . . maybe you should just turn around and try the back exit.

- **NO TURNING BACK NOW. IF YOU CHOOSE THE FRONT EXIT, TURN TO PAGE 165.**
- **THIS IS WAY TOO RISKY. IF YOU TURN AROUND TO GO OUT THE BACK EXIT, TURN TO PAGE 167.**

"That's really cool! Hercules fought that crazy-looking monster?" you ask. You've obviously heard of Hercules before, he's some kind of ancient hero. Plus, there are, like, a million movies about him. But you realize you don't actually know that much about the guy. Just his name, really.

You lean in to look more closely at the book's cover. The monster makes you think a bit about those old kaiju movies Dad likes so much. You feel a pit in your stomach when you remember what happened to him. You feel extra worse that for one small moment you actually forgot about it. That's maybe the worst part about horrible things happening—life also happens. And sometimes life makes you forget the horrible thing. And then that just makes you feel super guilty.

"Yeah, Hercules has all these challenges he has to do, and one of them is fighting a Hydra that regrows its heads when he chops them off! It feels impossible to defeat it, but then he thinks his strategy through and realizes he has to solder the necks shut with fire so they don't grow back. He was a warrior but also a super cool problem solver." She's really into telling you all these details, and her enthusiasm is contagious.

"I really like that," you say and you smile at each other. Could it be you've made a new friend?

The bell rings and lunch is over. You walk back to the school building together, agreeing to make your lunch hang a regular thing.

It's really nice to know that even with Ben gone you can make a new friend. And someone who actually lives in your time.

Shoot, that pit-in-the-stomach feeling is back. Dad. Gone. Rabbit. At home. Kids. Dead.

Why does your life have to be a living nightmare? Why can't you ever just be a normal kid?

➤ TURN TO PAGE 78.

The school day ends all too quickly. As the clock ticks away above the door, you realize that very soon you'll have to return to your house and the whole rabbit situation. That Dad is still missing and you've done absolutely nothing to find him. You've wasted a day relearning all the things you supposedly forgot over the summer, except you never did. You should have skipped the first day back and just gone right to Jeff's after the rabbit dropped you off. That would have been the smart decision.

Man, you've never felt quite so stupid as you have these past twenty-four hours.

As you walk down the front steps of the school, you hope that maybe Dad will appear to pick you up. Or maybe no one will come and you can walk home. Or run away. Or something.

But sure enough, there it is, that terrifying rabbit, waiting for you at the drop-off spot, sitting behind the wheel of the car. This time the place is swarming with kids, and you look around to see if any of them notice the rabbit in the driver's seat. But no one seems to notice. Or, at the very least, seems to care. You feel like a rabbit mascot in a car would be a big hit for kids, and you think maybe this means that only you can see it. Maybe you are the only one who is meant to. Or maybe you truly *are* going crazy.

How do you know if you are just seeing things? How do you know if anything is real?

You don't exactly have time to think about that kind of thing. And you're still trying to keep the creature as calm as possible so you get in the car and let it drive you home. The second you get inside, you dash up to your room, shut the door behind you, and this time drag your desk chair in front of it for good measure.

You throw your backpack on the bed and land beside it with a similar *thump*. You lie there for a moment, trying to think what you should do. Your mind is a blank. You decide to reach for your bag and maybe try to do homework or something. Anything to get your brain working again. You open your bag.

- JUST YOUR BOOKS AND YOUR HOMEWORK. UGH, NO, THERE IS NO WAY YOU CAN DO HOMEWORK. IF YOU CHANGE YOUR MIND AND CLOSE THE BAG, TURN TO PAGE 80.
- IF YOU SEE THE BUNNY EARS YOU WON BACK IN 1985, TURN TO PAGE 129.
- IF YOU SEE THE FLASHLIGHT YOU WON BACK IN 1985, TURN TO PAGE 80.

So you lie there. You let your eyes get fuzzy and you let all your thoughts wash over you. You don't grab at any in particular, you just sort of watch them as they float by. You're kind of tired of your thoughts, if you're honest. You'd be really happy not to think for a while.

Time passes and your stomach rumbles. It must be getting close to dinnertime, and living nightmare or not, you're still a human who needs to eat. *Do rabbit mascots need to eat?* You shake off the thought and sit up. Okay, you'll go downstairs, just quickly eat something. You need your strength to survive all this.

So, you push your desk chair to the side, open your door, and go downstairs to the kitchen. The rabbit has heated up some microwave dinners that your family only eats for emergencies. Another clear sign this is *so* not your Dad. If the whole large yellow rabbit mascot thing wasn't evidence enough.

"Hey," you say, trying to be chill and feeling anything but.

Of course, the rabbit doesn't say anything back. You glance down its open mouth, hoping to see the person inside the costume, just once. But again all you see is blackness.

You eat your food. Then you wonder if anyone has given anything to Jinx in a while. You couldn't imagine the rabbit would. You wonder if she's come out from hiding at all today.

"I'm, uh, just going to take some milk up to Jinx," you say as if the rabbit cares.

You head back upstairs, careful not to spill the milk. Jinx slinks up to you from her hiding spot, and you and she go into the safety of your room. You put the bowl down for her and she laps at it hungrily.

Yup, it seems everyone is a little hungry right now. Stupid rabbit.

Stupid, terrifying, horrific rabbit.

You feel this spark deep inside you flare up again. You can't live another day like this, it's too crazy and too awful. You have to save

Dad. Tonight you'll sneak out and save him. That's all there is to it! You'll do it tonight, late when Mom and that . . . thing . . . are asleep. You'll sneak out and rescue Dad and everything will be okay again!

Time passes stupidly slowly and you can't even get any sleep. Any time you do try to close your eyes, sudden flashes of the animatronic band rush forward into your brain. Like the worst kind of horror movie jump scare. So you just lie there staring at the ceiling. Straining your ears to hear sounds from below. Waiting for complete silence.

You look at the clock. It's 10 p.m. That's late enough.

You sit up and grab at your backpack, since that's what you usually do.

➤ IF YOU HAVE A PAIR OF BUNNY EARS IN YOUR BACKPACK, TURN TO PAGE 86.
➤ IF YOU DON'T HAVE ANY BUNNY EARS, TURN TO PAGE 82.

It's time to go. Stop procrastinating! The house has been still and silent for forever now. And the longer you wait, the more you risk something weird happening. You put the bag down and get up carefully and quietly. You have no idea where the rabbit is in the house, but you know it wouldn't be happy with you rescuing your dad. Hopefully, it's still sleeping in Dad's room. Regardless, you will need to be sneaky.

You tiptoe across your room to your door and see that Jinx has fallen asleep in front of it. A very cute if useless guard. She's in a tight little ball, holding the tip of her tail between her two front paws. You can't help but smile—you don't want to bother her.

➤ **IF YOU DECIDE TO GO AROUND JINX, TURN TO PAGE 134.**

➤ **IF YOU DECIDE TO STEP OVER JINX, TURN TO PAGE 87.**

You run over to the cake and quickly start cutting it into pieces. This is madness! You glance over your shoulder—the rabbit is still coming for you; it's now halfway across the room. Thank goodness it somehow doesn't seem to know how to run. As you serve the first piece of cake, you feel ridiculous, but for some reason, now you kind of feel like this is the right choice. It calms you down a bit even as you sense the rabbit's imminent arrival.

You continue to serve.

Cake.

Cake.

Cake.

And . . . final piece of cake to the girl with curly hair.

You stand over the kids as in unison they all dig into their slices and take a bite. As they chomp down on the cake, you can't help but look over at the rabbit again. Is it here yet? Is it going to attack you all?

You notice instead that it's stopped in place. Well, that's good at least.

Then it starts to convulse, like it's being electrocuted or something. It spasms and flinches and bounces in place. And then, right in front of you, in front of the kids, in front of the cake, it explodes into a million pieces!

Instinctively you crouch and hide your head under your arms, bracing yourself against the flying pixels, but they miraculously avoid you and the kids. You look up and the coast is clear. The kids are cheering. The word "Yay" appears over their heads.

And then a giant blue "Winner" appears. It's so big you worry it's going to fall on you and crush you. But then you realize: *Oh, 'winner.'*

Suddenly the world rushes around you again, that colorful *whoosh* like at the start of the game. You understand in this whirlwind that you've won the game. You are quite proud of yourself!

The whooshing stops and you steady yourself. You are standing in front of the arcade game again. And the game is so totally real, not made up of pixels or anything! You quickly look at your hands and are more than relieved that they are your hands. Real human flesh and blood and bone—and all the other stuff people are made of—hands. You can't help but smile.

You look up and realize you aren't in the past anymore. You are back in Jeff's Pizza. But since when did Jeff's have old-fashioned arcade games? It's then that you hear the noise. The din of customers enjoying their food. You look around and see the booths are full, there are a couple of waiters running around delivering sodas, and Jeff looks happy and satisfied behind his counter. Still kind of greasy, but a lot less pathetic-looking.

As for you, well, you're standing in a corner with three other arcade games against the wall. You realize only then that you're where the ball pit used to be. But there's no ball pit anymore. Just happy, colorful video games. On the wall beside where you're standing is a framed newspaper article. You read the headline: "Kids Saved from Certain Death! Whole Town Rejoices!" There's a picture of a person in a mascot suit being handcuffed by police. And five kids watching with their parents. There is a date, too. 1985.

1985?

Wait . . . did you do that?

"Hey, Oswald, having fun?"

You jump and turn. It's Dad. "Uh yeah, I think . . . I think I beat the game." And saved the lives of five kids. And . . . changed the course of history?

"Sweet, good job! Wanna challenge your old man?"

You look at him. You're supposed to be mad at him, you remember that now. But he seems to have forgotten about any of your arguments. And honestly, after everything you've just been through with those kids, well, you kind of think it's silly to be fighting about stupid stuff. Plus, taking care of kids is hard work. They can be really annoying even when you're trying to help them. You feel like you understand Dad's perspective a lot better now.

And playing a game together would be fun.

You look down at the flashing "Start" on *8-Bit Escape* and think, *Maybe not this one*. You don't want to undo everything. After all, you're a hero. Not that anyone will ever know that.

"Uh, maybe *Donkey Kong* instead?" You gesture at the game beside you.

"Bad choice there, kid, I'm a *Donkey Kong* grand master!" Dad rolls up his sleeves.

You shake your head and laugh. "You wish," you say.

You play the game together and it's a lot of fun. You feel bad about being annoyed and frustrated with Dad—after all, he is just trying to do his best.

You enjoy some pizza together and take a pie to-go for Mom.

All differences are set aside, and it actually turns into a pretty fantastic summer.

> ACHIEVEMENT UNLOCKED—SECRET ENDING

> THE END

There are those darn bunny ears, still sticking up from behind your gym shorts. They look even more ridiculous now than before. You have that same thought you had earlier—*If you put them on, maybe the rabbit will leave you alone*. That same crazy thought. Nothing else seems to have worked, so maybe it's time for some crazy?

- **NO, IT'S NOT. IF YOU DON'T PUT THEM ON, TURN TO PAGE 82.**
- **IT'S TIME. IF YOU PUT THEM ON, TURN TO PAGE 132.**

Jinx wakes up and blinks sleepily as you pass over her. She looks a little annoyed that you've woken her up. She slumps off to go sleep safely under the bed. You're happy she's hiding herself. You don't want to have to worry about her safety, too! Well . . . when it comes to Jinx, maybe the rabbit should be the worried one. She's little, but she can be scrappy. It's one of the many things you love about her.

You turn back to the door and take in a deep breath. Then you carefully turn the doorknob and pull your door open, inch by inch, slowly and carefully. You're proud that you don't make a sound as you enter the hallway. You just have to keep this up for a little longer! Take things one step at a time and make it downstairs.

You walk slowly down the hall toward the top of the staircase but then notice the bathroom.

➤ IF YOU DECIDE TO USE THE BATHROOM BEFORE YOU LEAVE, TURN TO PAGE 88.

➤ IF YOU SKIP THE BATHROOM AND HEAD DOWNSTAIRS, TURN TO PAGE 90.

You head quietly to the bathroom, but once you're in there you change your mind and realize you really don't want to risk using it because you'll make noise flushing the toilet and running the tap. They might be normal nighttime noises, but right now you actually think *any* noise is probably a bad idea. You don't want the rabbit to even remember you are in the house at all, let alone question if your late-night bathroom habits are sincere or not.

You take a moment to gather yourself and plan your next move. You stare at your reflection in the mirror on the medicine cabinet. You didn't turn the bathroom light on so you are lit from the side by the streetlight outside the window. It creates weird shadows across your face. You look tired but also not like you. Like a weird distorted monster version of you.

You shake your head to rid it of that thought and quickly open the medicine cabinet to hide from the mirror. All the usual stuff is there: toothpaste, toothbrushes, Tylenol, Dad's razor. And Jinx's syringes and medicine that you give her to make her sleep when you are traveling long distances with her. She gets really anxious and upset otherwise. Poor thing.

- **YOU SIGH AND CLOSE THE MEDICINE CABINET DOOR. IF YOU HEAD DOWNSTAIRS, TURN TO PAGE 90.**
- **YOU HAVE AN IDEA THAT MAYBE YOU COULD USE JINX'S MEDICINE ON THE RABBIT. IF YOU GRAB A SYRINGE, TURN TO PAGE 89.**

As quietly as possible, so quiet that it makes every small sound echo loudly like a rock tossed down a hollow well, you creep into your parents' bedroom. There's the rabbit, lying on the bed, its head on Dad's pillow. Mom still hasn't come home from the hospital. It must have been a tough shift.

You look at the rabbit carefully, trying to examine the situation. It's really hard to assess what's up with a mascot. They always look exactly the same, and their eyes don't close when they sleep. But the rabbit is unmoving and its breathing seems slow and measured. Maybe it actually is asleep? How can you know for sure?

You're suddenly not so confident about your plan. The idea of entering the room, crossing over to your dad's side of the bed, and stabbing this creature with a syringe seems incredibly, stupidly dangerous now. Do you try to drug the rabbit regardless of your fear?

➤ IF NO, TURN TO PAGE 90.
➤ IF YES, TURN TO PAGE 142.

You assess the staircase in front of you as it disappears into the dark void of downstairs. Has it always had this many stairs? Has it always looked this steep? Why does a simple set of stairs you've used every day your whole life suddenly look like some intimidating obstacle out of a high-level video game? And how are you supposed to approach going down them without making a sound and drawing the attention of a freaky rabbit?

- **IF YOU DECIDE TO GO DOWN THEM AS QUICKLY AS YOU CAN, TURN TO PAGE 112.**
- **IF YOU KEEP WITH THE PLAN OF TAKING EVERYTHING SUPER SLOW AND CAREFUL, TURN TO PAGE 143.**

You're getting kind of good at this going carefully and staying quiet thing as you move as quickly as you think is safe down the hall to the kitchen and then to the back door on your toes. You hold your breath as you open the door, but it's always been nice and quiet and doesn't let you down. No creaks here! Thank goodness. You step out into the cool evening air and shut the door as carefully and quietly as possible, hoping it doesn't click too loudly.

You glance up at the window on the second floor. The one belonging to Mom and Dad's room. Or Mom and the rabbit's room now? No, that's just not a thing, and definitely *won't* be a thing after tonight. After you rescue Dad.

You make your way down the side of the house to the street and then . . . well, then you start to run.

You just turn right and race out onto the dark street. You don't look behind you to see if the rabbit has figured out you've escaped yet. Instead, you just focus on the pools of light from the streetlamps, dashing as fast as you can from one pool to the next, desperately avoiding the shadows.

You've never been that great at gym class or anything, but the need to rescue Dad and your fear of that stupid rabbit keep you running the whole way to Jeff's. Coach García would be proud! You don't really even realize you've run that far until you arrive outside Jeff's door. You're panting hard and sweat is pouring down your brow. Is this what it feels like to do sports? It's kind of exhilarating you guess but also, kind of the worst. You try to catch your breath as you go inside Jeff's. You didn't actually worry it might be closed so late at night until you enter and realize, *Wow, Jeff's stays open late. For what customers, exactly?* you wonder. But you're not going to question something that you are so grateful for.

What would you have done if he'd been closed? Break a window? Unlikely.

Jeff looks at you funny. "We only serve whole pies at night," he says.

Oh right, you need an excuse for being there.

"I just wanted a soda."

Yeah, that's totally believable. What kid crosses town and shows up at a pizza place just to order a single soda? You inwardly roll your eyes at yourself.

But Jeff just shrugs and goes back into the kitchen. "Gotta put the next pie in the oven; I'll be back."

Really it's more than you could have asked for, because the second he disappears is the second you dash over to the ball pit. You stop yourself short, realizing you shouldn't just dive into it, you might be sent to 1985 and the murder restaurant. So you crouch down and lean over the edge of the pit, rummaging as much as you can through the balls. He has to be in here, surely he's in here! You're terrified Dad is in 1985, and then what will you do?

It's not working. You can't feel anything. You have no choice—you have to go into the pit. You have to follow tradition. If you end up in the past, well, hopefully Dad's there, too.

You dive into the pit and the balls cover you up, filling in any space and making you feel really claustrophobic in here for the first time. You think it's probably not about the ball pit itself, it's probably just you feeling trapped in the whole situation. A kind of metaphor. And then you realize you haven't started to count to a hundred yet and you really can't waste time thinking about all this stuff.

So you start to count to a hundred, and you just tell yourself you won't climb out of the pit or anything. You'll avoid the risk of 1985 and stay safe under here and just keep looking for Dad. And when you find *him*, immediately count to a hundred again.

One hundred.

You wait to hear the sounds of 1985. You hope for the beeps and dings of arcade games, but you fear the screams.

Instead you feel something hard against your back and you spin in place. You reach out for it—a boot. You reach along the boot and feel an ankle. The sensation when you discover it is like being electrocuted! Dad? Oh, you hope it is. There's a leg and a torso and then you reach up for his face and hope it's a real one and not some stupid mascot head and you take a deep breath. You feel skin and stubble, it seems so familiar, it has to be Dad, it has to be! You quickly count to a hundred again.

Then it's time to get the two of you out of this pit!

You've read stories about moms lifting whole cars off their kids, how adrenaline does crazy things to the human body. Heck, it made you run nonstop to Jeff's! But as you pull and pull at who you really hope is Dad, you are struck by your ability to rise to the surface with him in your grasp. You emerge out of the ball pit, mercifully at Jeff's, and pull the body behind you. It's so heavy, yet somehow you're doing it. You drag the torso up above the balls, it feels impossible but you do it. You turn to look at it. It is Dad! It's him! You found him!

Oh please don't be dead, Dad, please! I'm so sorry for all our fights, they were so stupid! You think all this as you press your head to his chest, listening for a heartbeat. You think you can hear it. You hope you can hear it and it's not you just wanting it to be there.

You sit up and look at Dad in the pit. How can you get him out of there and take him home? Jeff will probably find this all super weird but he'd help, right? Well . . . it's hard to say, really. He might just shrug and then go back into the kitchen like he pretty much does with everything. You know you should probably call Mom, but would she be mad? After all, the last time you texted her, she didn't believe anything was wrong. Would it be the same now? The boy who cried rabbit?

Suddenly you are grabbed from behind by a pair of yellow fuzzy arms. You flail and twist and kick, you are picked up in the air and turned around, but your fighting back seems to have worked and it loses its grip on you. You escape and stare up, knowing full well what attacked you. The rabbit has found you!

- **NOT THIS TIME, RABBIT! IF YOU RUSH AT IT WITH YOUR OWN ATTACK, TURN TO PAGE 113.**
- **IF YOU DIVE BACK INTO THE PIT, TURN TO PAGE 155.**

Every head that Hercules cut off grew back twofold, and he still kept fighting until he solved how to defeat the beast. Now is no time to give up. You just have to rally, fight back, until you win! Because you are the hero, and heroes *win*!

With your other arm you take a mighty swing and clock the rabbit right in the head. It doesn't knock it out or anything, but it shakes it up enough that it releases the grip on your arm. You pull away and prepare to fight the beast, but it doesn't pursue you. Instead it suddenly turns its focus on Dad, lying there unconscious in the ball pit. The rabbit's jaws are wide like a snake, its teeth dripping with your blood, ready to inhale your dad whole.

Well, that's not going to happen!

You don't care about the throbbing pain in your arm, and your good friend adrenaline is seriously on your side right now because you launch yourself again at the rabbit, using the netting to spring yourself forward. As you fly in the air onto the rabbit's back, you cry out: "Leave my dad alone!"

Not as cool as some action movie one-liners, but it comes from a place deep inside your very soul, and as you land on the rabbit's back, you start pummeling its head, hard. You reach around and claw at its plastic eyes. You are determined to stop this thing no matter what.

The rabbit twists and turns under your attack, and then with an otherworldly almost mechanical roar it throws you off and into the pit. You land hard next to your unconscious dad, and you scramble to pull yourself back out for round two. This fight isn't over until you say it's over!

As you burst out from the balls, you're struck by the sight in front of you. Somehow the twisting and throwing you off its back has caught the rabbit up in the netting, one rope around its throat, pulling it up dangling above the floor. The more it twists, the more the rope tightens and you just watch in horror and awe . . .

And then.

Stillness.

Nothing but an old dirty yellow rabbit mascot suit hanging limp from a rope around its neck.

A sudden gasp and you wheel around in the pit to find Dad has opened his eyes and taken in a deep breath. You rush over to him, thrilled beyond anything that he's awake. That he's alive!

Dad looks around, confused. "I don't understand why I'm here. What's happening . . ." He finally makes eye contact with you and his panic starts to melt. He looks so tired but so happy to see you. "What happened?"

What happened? *Oh you know, the usual, a giant yellow rabbit kidnapped you and took your place, and I fought it and it hanged itself.* Yeah, no, that sounded crazy. And considering the fact that Jinx seems to be the only other creature alive that has been able to see the rabbit, probably very hard to prove.

So instead you shoulder the blame. "So, uh . . . I hid in the ball pit to play a prank on you, which I shouldn't have done. You came to look for me, and I guess you must've hit your head and lost consciousness." And even though none of that was true, there is one thing that is: "I'm sorry, Dad. I didn't mean for things to get so out of hand."

You really, really didn't.

Dad pushes himself up to sitting with a heavy grunt and moves his head back and forth, twisting his neck a little bit. "I accept your apology, son," he says with a tired smile. "But you're right—you shouldn't have done it. And Jeff really should get rid of this ball pit before he has a lawsuit on his hands."

Well, that was something you definitely could agree on. You help Dad to stand and you both climb out of the pit.

You see Dad notice something, and you turn to where he's looking. The rabbit costume. Hanging there. Lifeless.

"What's that creepy thing?"

And you answer honestly: "I have no idea."

Dad turns to look at you—maybe he doesn't quite believe you? That's when he sees your arm. "Oswald! Are you okay?"

It hurts, sure, but you are so okay, better than okay. Dad's back! "I'm fine," you say.

"Uh-huh. We're getting you home so your mom can look at that."

You seriously have no issues with that suggestion.

You make your way to the exit, and you just feel so happy Dad's okay and also super guilty about all your arguments this summer.

"Dad, I know I can be a pain sometimes, but I really do love you, you know."

Dad looks at you, pleased but a little surprised. You don't blame him. It does probably feel super out of nowhere that you've said that.

"Same here, kiddo." He reaches over to ruffle your hair. "But you do have terrible taste in science fiction movies."

You laugh. "Oh, yeah? Well, you have terrible taste in music. And you like boring ice cream."

"My taste is impeccable. Refined."

"Sure, if boring means refined."

You both laugh and you grab Dad and give him a side hug. He squeezes you tightly back. "Now let's go home and watch one of my terrible movies," he says.

"It's a plan!"

As the door to Jeff's closes behind you and you breathe in the cool, clean night air, you hear Jeff call out, "Hey, kid! You forgot your soda!"

➤ IF YOU HAVE HALF OR A WHOLE GOLDEN TOKEN, TURN TO PAGE 98.

➤ IF YOU DON'T HAVE ANY PIECES OF A GOLDEN TOKEN, TURN TO PAGE 111.

As you walk down the street with your dad, you actually enjoy the quiet stillness of your small town for once. You look around, appreciating the tiny main street and how the streetlamps make it look a bit like a scene out of a movie. You notice something glint in one of the lights as you approach. You bend down and see half a golden token on the ground. You pick it up and notice that you are standing next to a wall of windows, boarded up like they always are. This is that extended arcade games area that used to be a part of Freddy's.

You shake your head and can't quite believe everything you've been through this summer. You look closer at the coin.

- **IF IT LOOKS LIKE THE OTHER HALF YOU HAVE IN YOUR POCKET, TURN TO PAGE 99.**
- **IF YOU ALREADY HAVE A WHOLE COIN IN YOUR POCKET, TURN TO PAGE 104.**

Yup, it's exactly like the other half in your pocket. As you pick up your pace to catch up to Dad, you pull the other half out and sure enough the two halves snap together seamlessly.

You put the now-whole token in your pocket and continue your walk home with Dad, feeling content and happy.

THE END

➤ **ADD THE <u>GOLD TOKEN</u> BONUS ITEM TO YOUR INVENTORY, AND TURN TO PAGE 2 FOR A BRAND-NEW ADVENTURE.**

You wait as you always do for Dad to pick you up. The wait just makes your anger grow stronger and stronger. You become more and more annoyed with him, his stupid job, his stupid taste in music, his insistence that somehow going to the library and then for pizza is the ultimate summer vacation. He doesn't understand. He doesn't know what it's like to be stuck in a town like this. When he was a kid there were arcades and stuff—you know, he's told you about it!

By the time he picks you up, you're fuming. You climb into the passenger seat and slam the door behind you.

"Hey, champ, don't slam the door, okay?" Dad says.

"I hate when you call me champ. And who cares about a stupid car door?" you reply, totally pissed off.

"I care. I have to pay for it if it breaks—you should have more respect for things."

"Respect for this hunk of junk?"

"Cut it out, you're being very disrespectful," replied Dad with his serious voice.

You hate his serious voice.

"Yeah, because you totally respect me," you scoff.

"I do!"

"You don't!"

"I do!"

You are so busy arguing that Dad has turned to look at you and he doesn't see the red light on the only set of streetlights in town. And of course the one time a car is actually coming from the other direction, it has to be now.

GAME OVER

>TO TRY AGAIN TURN TO PAGE 2

You put on the hat, placing the elastic around your chin, feeling it dig into your skin. You start to feel even more dizzy. The room is kind of spinning now and you find it hard to stay standing. Like you've spun very fast in a circle and then stopped. That strange numb feeling you were feeling is now all kind of floaty. It's even more dreamlike but also different. Like you aren't even *you* asleep dreaming. More like you are in someone else's dream. Observing it . . . from a far distance. You don't feel like Oswald. You don't even feel like a person, really.

You find yourself following the rabbit down a hall. Where did this hall come from? You turn to see a door shutting closed behind you. The sounds of the arcade are silenced in the cold empty gray of the stark hallway. You turn and continue following the rabbit. It's not even like you are walking, you're just kind of floating except your feet are firmly planted on the ground.

- **SOMETHING DEEP IN YOUR GUT IS TELLING YOU THIS IS BAD. YOU NEED TO MAKE IT BACK TO THAT DOOR. IF YOU TURN AROUND TO TRY TO LEAVE, TURN TO PAGE 102.**
- **IF YOU JUST KEEP FOLLOWING THE RABBIT, TURN TO PAGE 103.**

The whole hallway keels to the side, and then you realize—no, it's you doing the keeling. You grab at the hat on your head and try to pull it off your head. Your fingers feel clumsy, or maybe you're wearing mitts? In the middle of summer? Yeah, that makes sense.

You manage to tear the hat off your head, and the spinning stops. It's like someone has splashed cold water on your face and you don't waste any time. You start to sprint back to the door and away from the rabbit. You only manage to take one step before it grabs you from behind. You feel sharp pain and confusion, you cry out, and panic takes over. Another sharp pain, so sharp that you can't even scream. So sharp it digs deep inside you to the core of your very soul.

GAME OVER

>TO TRY AGAIN TURN TO PAGE 2

You continue to follow the rabbit. What other choice do you have? After all, this isn't your dream, and you're at the mercy of someone else's thoughts. Whatever the dreamer wants, you have to do. Somewhere you know that's a ridiculous idea, but it also feels very accurate.

The rabbit leads you to another gray metal door. Have you gone in a complete circle? Is this the arcade again?

It opens the door and you find that you are entering a large storage closet back room kind of place. Interesting. There are old toys on shelves, a mop and bucket in the corner, and a kid sitting on the ground also wearing a birthday hat. You blink slowly as the door closes behind you. *Oh,* you think to yourself, *would you look at that. The kid's dead.*

You turn to ask if the rabbit knows why the kid is dead.

It makes you into another dead kid.

GAME OVER

>TO TRY AGAIN TURN TO PAGE 2

Yup, it's exactly like the whole token in your pocket, except only one half of it. Weird. As you pick up your pace to catch up to Dad, you put the half in your pocket. Why not?

You continue your walk home with Dad, feeling content and happy.

THE END

➤ ADD THE GOLD TOKEN BONUS ITEM TO YOUR INVENTORY, AND TURN TO PAGE 2 FOR A BRAND-NEW ADVENTURE.

You all think the flashlight is actually a pretty cool prize for a place like this, and you pack it away in your backpack.

The conversation turns to movies, but you keep glancing over to the corner, looking at the rabbit.

"Seriously? You liked *The Eternal Song*? It was so boring," Mike is saying. You're not really paying attention.

"Oh, come on, it's good! You just have crap taste. Right, Oz?" Chip says.

You hear your new nickname, but it doesn't fully register until he asks you again.

"Oh, uh, yeah."

"Dude!" says Mike.

"What?"

Chip is laughing. "See, he agrees you have crap taste!"

Shoot, you hadn't actually heard the question. Now you feel bad.

"Well, what movies do you like, then?" asks Mike, scoring in air hockey. The lights flash and there's the sound of the recorded cheering of a crowd.

You realize this is a complicated question. You could say you like those old monster movies, since those are even older than the '80s, but if you say that, they might think you're a huge nerd. But you can't say any movies from after 1985, and it's not like you keep track of exact movie dates. You decide to take a swing and hope you're right: "Uh, *E.T.*?"

"Dude, that's, like, from three years ago! You need to seriously get out more! Do they not have movie theaters where you're from?"

Sure they do, they also have Netflix and YouTube and TikTok . . . but you can't tell them that, of course.

"It's still a good movie," you say quietly. You're embarrassed and so used to being bullied for your tastes you can feel your cheeks turning red.

"Yeah, it totally is, but let's make a plan to see a new movie together so we can get you into the future!" says Chip with a smile.

You look at him. No mean comment? Just quick teasing and then a plan to hang out more? You're not used to this. You wish you could actually go to a movie theater with these guys.

Well, maybe you can. You don't actually know if you're able to leave the arcade or not. There's a thought. Could you explore the whole 1985 version of your town? Could you go farther? Like, to a big city like New York or L.A.? Could you see what the whole world was like in 1985? And could you do it all and still be back at Jeff's in time for Dad to pick you up? The possibilities are kind of endless. Your mind is seriously blown. You could explore in the past and the present. Or, you suppose, Chip and Mike's future.

"Into the future?" you say with a bit of a smile. If only they knew . . .

"Okay, I'm scoping out the scene. I've got tokens on three games now, one of them has to be free—be right back!" says Chip.

"Yeah, I'll grab drinks. Oz?" asks Mike.

"I'm good."

And you really are. Better than good. For the first time in a long time, you feel like you actually belong. You lean against the air hockey table and look over at the rabbit. It's still staring at you. You're feeling pretty awesome now, pretty up for anything. Suddenly it raises a hand and crooks its finger at you in that "come here" kind of motion. You look over your shoulder. Is it signaling you? Looks like it. Super weird.

➤ **IF YOU DON'T FOLLOW THE RABBIT, TURN TO PAGE 38.**

➤ **IF YOU FOLLOW THE RABBIT, TURN TO PAGE 107.**

You walk over to the rabbit. You feel a little lightheaded now, almost like you are walking in a dream. All the kids making noise around you kind of vanishes in your mind, and your only focus is on the weird rabbit mascot guy. The dead eyes stay on you the whole time. You are drawn to them, even as they seem more soulless as you get closer.

It's all so strange.

"Hi," you say when you arrive.

The rabbit doesn't say anything back.

What a weird mascot.

"So . . . you're a rabbit, huh?" It's a pretty stupid thing to say, but you're feeling kind of stupid. Kind of numb, honestly. Like there's this empty well inside you, but you are also inside it.

Okay, that was a trippy thought.

The rabbit turns and opens the door it's standing next to. It looks back at you. *Oh, it wants me to follow,* you think.

Maybe you shouldn't, but you kind of want to. So you do.

You find yourself following the rabbit through the door and down a dull gray hallway. You're not sure why you're doing it. Yes, you are a little curious, but it doesn't feel like curiosity is motivating you forward.

Suddenly, the rabbit turns quickly, too quickly for a normal person in a clunky mascot costume. It lunges at you in some kind of attack, opening its mouth wide and revealing sharp, spiky teeth.

Do you have the flashlight?!

➤ IF YES, TURN TO PAGE 108.

➤ IF NO, TURN TO PAGE 110.

Instinct takes over and washes away any of that weird empty feeling. You are alert and you brandish the only thing you've got that's close to a weapon: the flashlight. You turn it on and shine it directly into the rabbit's face. You expect it to raise its arms to shield itself from the light or to stumble a bit in the brightness. What you don't expect is for it to fall backward, hit its head, and start to convulse. Its whole body starts shaking like there's an earthquake. It staggers and stumbles and falls into a pile of garbage waiting by the back door. You should run, but you stand there instead, perfectly still, waiting for the rabbit's next move. It lies there, lifeless, and that's when you see red spreading across the suit. You realize what has happened. It's been impaled on something.

You don't waste another moment! You turn as fast as you can and run away. You rush through the door back into the restaurant and your senses are assaulted by all the noise and lights. What was once a pleasant exciting atmosphere now feels chaotic and disturbing. You don't bother to look for Chip or Mike. You have only one goal: to get home, to get back to your time. To boring Jeff's. To boring Dad. To your boring life.

Oh man, boring sounds amazing just about now.

You race across the restaurant to the ball pit.

But it's gone.

It's like it never existed.

In its place is a small party area and a group of little kids celebrating a birthday at a table. There is cake and plates, and the kids are all wearing party hats.

You wheel around. Where is it? It has to be somewhere. Anywhere! But you can't see it.

You're trapped. In 1985. Forever.

GAME OVER

>TO TRY AGAIN TURN TO PAGE 2

You race toward the back exit door as fast as your feet can carry you and fly through it. The harsh light of day blinds you for a moment, but you blink hard several times and are able to finally acclimate to the brightness. You look around. The door has slammed shut with a *bang* behind you, thank goodness—this gives you a chance to find your bearings.

Though you can't take too long since the rabbit can burst out of there at any moment, you just know it!

You're in an alley that leads out onto Main Street. There's a dumpster and other doors to other buildings on each side. The brick walls on either side are tagged with graffiti and someone has drawn a one-eyed fox with a hook for a hand. He looks a bit like a pirate. There's a very specific smell of urine in the air.

And something else. A sound.

You strain to hear it. It sounds like someone is calling out to you. It's so faint and hard to hear, but you think it sounds very much like a kid.

Like a little girl.

You strain harder to listen. "Please, help me." It's so faint and quiet, but now that you understand it, you can hear it clearly.

You look over your shoulder, anticipating a rabbit attack from that door at any moment.

Do you really have the time to find and help this girl?

- **YOU DON'T. YOU FEEL TERRIBLE, BUT YOU NEED TO KEEP GOING. IF YOU QUICKLY RUN TOWARD THE STREET, TURN TO PAGE 117.**
- **YOU CAN'T JUST DO NOTHING. IF YOU DECIDE TO FOLLOW THE SOUND, TURN TO PAGE 114.**

You throw your hands up to protect your face, but it does nothing against the razor-sharp teeth of the rabbit. It bites down hard.

GAME OVER

>TO TRY AGAIN TURN TO PAGE 2

As you walk down the street with your dad, you actually enjoy the quiet stillness of your small town for once. You look around, appreciating Main Street and how the streetlamps make it look a bit like a scene out of a movie. You notice something glint in one of the lights as you approach. You bend down and see half a golden token on the ground. You pick it up and notice that you are standing next to a wall of windows, boarded up like they always are. This is that extended arcade games area that used to be a part of Freddy's.

You shake your head and can't quite believe everything you've been through this summer. You put the half token back where you found it, and then you pick up your pace to catch up to Dad. Together you walk home happily, but you can't help but feel like something is missing . . .

THE END

You charge down the stairs into the dark below as fast as you can. Your footsteps sound crazy loud, and you almost tumble down the steps headfirst. But you manage to stay upright and land at the bottom. You stop yourself at the front door, standing as still as you can. You crane your neck to hear the rabbit's footsteps racing after you, coming in for the attack, but all you can hear is the thudding of your heart in your ears. You dare to glance over your shoulder. All you see is blackness at the top of the staircase. Your heart is still racing, though. What are you waiting for? It's time to get out of here!

You reach for the doorknob and then pause. A horrific reminder hits your brain just in the nick of time: The front door makes this high-pitched squeak when you open it. It's always been a comforting sound, a sign your mom's made it home safe late at night after a long shift. But tonight, well—tonight, it's a lot more ominous. And it could definitely attract the attention of a creepy rabbit. Maybe you should use the back door instead? But that could waste precious minutes!

- **TIME IS OF THE ESSENCE. IF YOU DECIDE TO JUST USE THE FRONT DOOR AS QUICKLY AS YOU CAN, TURN TO PAGE 149.**
- **IT'S NOT WORTH THE RISK. IF YOU TAKE THE EXTRA TIME TO CROSS THE HOUSE TO THE BACK DOOR, TURN TO PAGE 91.**

You spin to face the rabbit. It's standing between you and Dad still in the pit, looming at you like it likes to do. No. Not this time. *Not this time!* Your adrenaline is still coursing through you and you rush the rabbit, launching yourself at its lower half. If you can push it off-balance, maybe you can send it into the ball pit and back to 1985 where it belongs! It staggers back, not falling off its feet but into the netting surrounding the pit. The useless netting that you realize finally has served its purpose of keeping people at bay in the worst possible moment. The rabbit steadies itself and then with surprising speed lunges at you, pinning you against the wall by the pit. You struggle against its grip, but it has you held fast.

Then it opens its mouth. That stupid horrible mouth that you've been staring into to try to see the person inside. That thing? It suddenly starts to open wider and wider. Revealing yet more blackness and no humanity within whatsoever. The jaw unhinges revealing two rows of razor-sharp fangs. Your blood runs cold. You struggle as hard as you can against the rabbit's grip as it lunges for your throat. Somehow you manage to block it with your arm and the teeth drive deep into your skin, your flesh, hitting bone. It's pain unlike anything you've felt before and you cry out loudly. The blood drips down your arm and you feel yourself getting weaker, not only physically, but also mentally. Like your energy and will to fight back is seeping out of you, along with your blood.

You feel hopeless and scared.

And then . . . for some reason . . . you remember Gabrielle and her book.

➤ **IF YOU REMEMBER THE STORY OF THESEUS AND HIS STRING, TURN TO PAGE 156.**

➤ **IF YOU REMEMBER THE STORY ABOUT HERCULES AND THE HYDRA, TURN TO PAGE 95.**

You listen hard to follow the sounds of the girl crying for help. You walk slowly, your head tilted a little to aim your ear, trying to push out all other distractions and just focus on your sense of hearing.

"Please. Help me."

There it is! A little louder now. Just a little farther up the alley. You make your way to a pair of wooden doors that lead down into some kind of cellar. There doesn't appear to be a lock on them. Still, with your luck, they'll be impossible to open. You have to bend over and pull each door up with both hands. It's an awkward angle, as gravity is fighting you, and you've never been particularly strong. But the first door actually comes up a bit with your tug, and that small accomplishment makes you want to pull harder. And harder. You pull the door up enough that the gravity grabs it from the other side and it falls open, hard. You can see cement stairs and now you hear: "Hurry, please!"

You pull at the other door, and it's just as tough, but now you have confidence and you fling it open in half the time.

You stare down into the cellar. The cement stairs lead into darkness. Well, this isn't creepy at all.

"Are you coming?"

Well, there's no turning back now, you suppose.

You take a few steps down the stairs and your eyes are able to adjust to the darkness as more steps materialize before you.

Then you see her.

Or . . . it?

You stop on the third step down. About five more steps away, sitting in the shadow, you see a toy doll that resembles a little girl. She has red hair in pigtails and is wearing a red dress to match her hair. Her face, legs, and arms are bone white, and she has a bloodred nose and crimson circles on her cheeks. Her entire appearance is unnerving.

She is silent.

"Hello?" you call out. "Is anyone there?" Maybe the girl who owns the doll is trapped farther into the darkness.

"Please help me."

The voice sounds like it's coming from the doll, but that makes no sense. Then again, time-travel and creepy rabbit mascots also make no sense.

You are seriously freaked out, and you are so done with this rescue mission. Abort, abort!

You turn around.

The rabbit is there! Standing above you.

You stare at it for a moment, and then it shoves you. Hard. You fall down all the steps onto the cement floor, cracking your head against it. You can feel something wet and warm oozing from beneath you.

The rabbit starts to walk down the stairs toward you; backlit by the bright sunshine outside, he is a giant silhouette, looming.

You hear the sound of laughter beside you. High-pitched giggling. You turn your head to look at the doll. She sits there, perfectly still. But the laughter gets louder and louder.

Her head suddenly snaps to look at you.

You struggle to get away.

The rabbit is there. It attacks. You feel sharp cold pain and scream out.

GAME OVER

>TO TRY AGAIN TURN TO PAGE 2

There's no time to lose. You don't even bother running down to the street, to the sidewalk. No, you cut across your lawn, jump over the short hedges that separate the two houses, and barrel up the steps to the dark green front door of your neighbors. You knock loudly, insistently. Someone has to be home! Please, please let someone be home!

The door opens. But it's definitely not Mr. or Mrs. Brown.

Another mascot is standing in front of you.

This time it's not a rabbit but a large chicken.

"Chica," you say out loud. You've learned the names of the Freddy animatronic band members well by now. Freddy the bear, Bonnie the purple rabbit, and Chica . . . the chicken. Wearing that way-too-cheerful LET'S EAT bib and holding that way-too-pink cupcake with the eyes and buck teeth.

Chica cocks its head to the side as you stare in horror.

Slowly you back away, one foot behind the other, staring into the hollow empty eyes of the yellow bird. You look at the LET'S EAT slogan. There's something terrifyingly gruesome about that. You feel sick to your stomach. You don't know what's going on.

Maybe this truly is a nightmare. Maybe you'll wake up.

Wake up, Oswald, wake up!

Suddenly you are grabbed from behind by two very familiar yellow arms. You have almost no time to register what is happening as both the chick and the rabbit descend upon you.

All you feel is a terrible sharp pain, and the world swims in your vision.

GAME OVER

>TO TRY AGAIN TURN TO PAGE 2

You run out of the alley and find yourself in the middle of Main Street, out of breath and overwhelmed. You wheel in a circle in place. Everything looks the same but also a bit different. The old boarded-up buildings look clean and have shops in them. Windows are washed. The front of the arcade extends into the building next to where Jeff's Pizza is in the future. Or the present. Or whatever any of this is.

Suddenly time moves forward around you like someone pressed a fast-forward button. The world blurs and speeds past, and you can barely make out what you're seeing. Cars, and people, and day and night, over and over with dizzying haste. And then it stops.

You look around and see Jeff's is back. The arcade is boarded up. The windows and stores look dull and lifeless, just as you are familiar with. And yet you aren't annoyed by it all like you usually are because you realize: You are back in your own time. Relief washes over you and you walk over to Jeff's and onto the sidewalk.

But then.

Then.

You see a reflection of yourself in the window. Your hair has flecks of gray, and your hairline is so far up your forehead, it's basically at the back of your head. Your face is lined. It hits you hard then. Not only has the world around you aged, but so have you! You are now old—like in your forties!

Your stomach twists and turns in a panic. And then you see Dad coming to pick you up at the restaurant like he has every day this summer. You see him go inside and hear him ask where you are. You approach the pizzeria and go inside.

"What do you mean, he was here a minute ago? Where is he now?" Dad's looking a little panicked.

You have to say something, do something. You approach them.

"Okay, so I know this sounds weird, but I'm actually right here," you say to Jeff and Dad. They both stare at you like they have no idea who you are. "Look it's me, it's Oswald. I traveled through time." Even as you say it you don't need to see their freaked-out expressions. They think you're crazy, and honestly, you think you might be crazy, too.

"Sir, I think it's best if you left," Dad says in that tone he saves for serious moments.

"Dad, it's me!" you insist.

"Leave now," says Jeff. He has his phone at the ready to call the cops.

You don't know what to do other than to do what they say. So you leave and cross the street, hiding yourself behind a small group of trees to observe and wait. You watch as there is panic when you aren't found. Police come. Dad speaks to them. Jeff speaks to them. You wonder what Mom will think when she finds out about all this.

You can't do anything to help, even though you are probably the most helpful person in this town for all this. No one will believe you. You're not even sure *you* believe you.

So, you just continue to watch. To experience. To feel useless.

You observe it all.

Mom hears the news about you and is devastated. It seems like the whole town tried to find you. Posters go up and eventually fade. Your Dad is on the news.

You have become a missing person.

You are never found.

Even though you are right here.

You are right. Here.

You live your life from this point on as your older self with a different name and no one ever knows what happened to you.

GAME OVER

>TO TRY AGAIN TURN TO PAGE 2

You race down the front path to the sidewalk and then run as fast as you can down the street. The houses blur in your peripheral vision and you feel a bit like a cartoon character running down an infinite hallway of repeating tables and paintings. House after house, lawn after lawn, hydrant after hydrant. Man, Jeff's is quite far away on foot!

Your mind wanders to Dad. You can imagine him, floating in a pool of infinite balls, lying there like a drowned man. His face drained of color. His lips purple and cold. All alone because of you. Dead because of you.

No! No, you won't think like that! You shake your head and dart across the street. There's a loud screech and you wheel around to see a car slamming to a stop just in front of you. You stare at the driver, a man in his forties or so. He looks somehow familiar. I mean, that's not unusual since you know almost everyone in this town, but this is different somehow.

He leans his head out the driver's side window and says, "Get in!"

- **IF YOU DON'T KNOW WHY, BUT YOU GET IN, TURN TO PAGE 121.**
- **NO WAY, YOU DON'T HAVE TIME FOR THIS, AND ANYWAY, WHAT KIND OF KID JUST GETS INTO A STRANGER'S CAR? IF YOU DON'T GET IN, TURN TO PAGE 120.**

You start running again. You glance back and see the car is still sitting there, and the man is still staring at you. What on earth is that about? That's just creepy. Okay, add that to the list of all the creepy things that have happened to you recently. You shake your head and turn back to focus on your journey to Jeff's.

Once again your mind becomes full of morbid thoughts about your dad. And once again you are brought out of your reverie by the screeching of tires on pavement. You look up—is that guy following you? Great, another person out to get you. Just what you need right now. But it's not that guy anymore. It's the rabbit. In Dad's car.

You realize what is happening a little too late. You try to run, but the rabbit is faster. Of course it is, it's driving a freaking car! It pushes the pedal to the metal and comes barreling toward you.

GAME OVER

>TO TRY AGAIN TURN TO PAGE 2

You aren't exactly sure why, with everything else that's happened to you, you are suddenly trusting some random stranger telling you to "Get in!" but "Get in" you do and quickly close the passenger side door behind you. You turn to look at the man, and he's just staring at you. He has blond hair, receding a bit at the temples, and a weary expression. Like a man who's traveled around the world a few times and not been happy with what he's seen. The way he's looking at you is unnerving, almost as unblinking as the rabbit, and you are so not down for any more unblinking nonsense.

"What?" you ask, maybe a bit more harshly than you intended but who cares, really? With everything going on, a bit of directness and mistrust isn't such a bad thing.

"I'm just . . . I mean I'd heard the stories, but . . . to see you. It's proof, isn't it? Evidence."

Okay, so this guy is either crazy or on something.

"Nah, dude, not today." You turn to leave and he grabs your arm. You instantly flinch, and he releases it. Holding his hand up high in a kind of apologetic gesture.

"Oz, man, it's me. I'm sorry. Didn't mean to spook you."

No one calls you Oz. No one except . . . you look at that face. Lined, sunken cheeks, bags under the eyes. But beneath it all that familiar look. That something else. That gut instinct.

"Chip?" You say it and you don't believe it.

The man smiles. A tired smile, but a smile nonetheless. "Yeah, man, it's me."

Chip. From 1985. Chip with the fluffy big hair and the toothy grin. There's some of that grin in his smile, hidden a bit, but there. "You're old now," you say.

Chip smiles wide and he laughs. Wow, now he looks so much like 1985, it's freaky. "Yeah, it happens. You didn't age a bit."

"Well, yeah, this is like . . . my time." You realize how that might sound, like gibberish. How best to explain . . .

"Okay, this is weird but the ball pit is like a time machine, and I've been going to your time all summer, but really it's been this time the whole time."

Too much use of the word time, you think to yourself.

Chip nods. He doesn't seem weirded out by this story in the least.

"Yeah. I mean, I didn't know about the ball pit, but a lot of weird stuff happened back in 1985, and there was some strange time-jumping stuff, too. I didn't experience it personally, but it was kind of a crazy summer for us back then. An awful summer." His expression grows dark, and you remember the dead kids in the back room and nod. You know what he's talking about.

"Other people time-jumped?" you ask instead, not wanting to discuss the horror.

"A couple kids in my time went back. Don't know if it was in the ball pit. Or something else. But yeah. It all makes sense."

You sit in silence for a moment.

Then you feel a sudden rush of realization flow over you like a wave.

"The rabbit, I'm running from the rabbit."

"That yellow mascot dude?" asks Chip right away. Oh wow, you don't even have to catch him up, it seems.

"Yes!" You are almost too relieved, it's this feeling as if you've already rescued your dad and got rid of the rabbit. But none of that has happened yet. You can't relax yet. You need to still stay vigilant.

"The rabbit hurt my dad, and now he's somewhere in the ball pit at Jeff's. Jeff's is where Freddy's used to be," you explain. "And meanwhile the rabbit has taken over my dad's life and I don't know what it wants, but I'm pretty sure it wants to kill me or something. It's freaky, and I don't know what's going on."

Chip nods along to everything you're saying like he's heard it all before. His expression is serious and determined.

"That rabbit's bad news. Trust me, we all know that. I totally believe it's done that. Not the first time it has time-jumped, either. No one's managed to destroy it." He takes a deep breath and then exhales. "Not yet."

"It's terrifying."

"Oz, I've put together a team to take down the rabbit once and for all. We've been waiting for it to appear in town again, and well, it looks like it's now or never. We were meant to meet today. Will you join us and help us end it?"

- **"OH, HECK YES!" YOU SAY. YOU ARE SO READY FOR THIS! IF YOU JOIN CHIP'S TEAM, TURN TO PAGE 126.**
- **"I'M SORRY, I'M JUST A KID. I CAN'T DO IT. BUT I BELIEVE THAT YOU GUYS CAN!" IF YOU ARE SO RELIEVED THAT SOMEONE ELSE CAN TAKE OVER FROM HERE, TURN TO PAGE 130.**

"Huh, I've never heard of Theseus before, I don't think. Who's that?" you ask. You've obviously heard of Hercules, and he's been in a ton of movies and stuff. But this guy? No idea.

"I guess he's not as well-known as Hercules," agrees Gabrielle, and you smile. It's nice to have a kind of normal conversation, even though it's also really weird to have a normal conversation when everything in your life is anything but.

"Yeah."

"Well, from what I understand so far, Theseus was tasked with killing a Minotaur at the center of this huge cavernous maze called a labyrinth."

"A Minotaur?"

"A monster with a bull for a head and a human body," she explains. You can't help but think of your monster with a rabbit for a head.

"Oh cool." But it doesn't actually feel like it is.

"Anyway, Theseus becomes friends with the princess, Ariadne, and she gives him a string that he can unwind as he travels in the maze so he doesn't get lost. That's all I've read so far, but I think it's really interesting." She's super into telling you all this, and her enthusiasm is contagious.

"I really like that," you say and you smile at each other. Could it be you've made a new friend? "I like that string idea, it's super simple but really smart."

"Sometimes simple is the best solution!"

The bell rings and lunch is over. You walk back to the school building together, agreeing to make your lunch hang a regular thing.

It's really nice to know that even with Ben gone you can make a new friend. And someone who actually lives in your time.

Shoot, that pit in the stomach feeling is back. Dad. Gone. Rabbit. At home. Kids. Dead.

Why does your life have to be a living nightmare? Why can't you ever just be a normal kid?

➤ **TURN TO PAGE 78.**

The drive is long and winding, and you leave your bleached dusty town for rolling hills of patchy yellow fields and dry dirt. The long hot summer has made its mark here, too, and even though you're breathing in the artificial cold from the car AC vents, you can still smell that heavy heat in the air.

You turn down a dirt road that throws you around in your seat. The car skids a bit in the gravel as if it's on ice and then settles into worn tracks that make for a slightly smoother ride. You don't say anything to Chip this whole time. You don't know what to say.

"So when you said you didn't really see movies . . ." he says instead.

You can't help but smile.

"Oh yeah, that was tough to think of movies from 1985. I mean, it's weird—I actually do watch old movies, my dad . . ." You stop then. Thinking about Dad makes your stomach clench.

"Your dad?"

"Yeah, he likes old movies. But even older than 1985." You don't really feel like talking anymore.

"It's weird to think of the '80s as 'old,'" says Chip.

"Not really."

"Well, yeah, not for you. But someday someone's going to say now is old, and then you'll get it." Chip gives you a grin, but you're just feeling worse and worse. You feel like you've abandoned Dad. Like anything could have happened to him. That anything could be happening to him.

You think about your fights and how you always say his taste in music is terrible.

Probably the same as what Chip is saying—stuff was cool once, and now it isn't. And the stuff you like probably won't be cool someday.

Not that you ever liked anything because it was cool, anyway. And you do kind of like those old monster movies.

Man, you feel like crap.

The car turns down a driveway. Long and winding, with pine trees flanking each side. At least these are green, unlike the other kinds of trees that seem ready for fall with browning, yellowing leaves.

You finally pull up to a large barn, the kind that's one-story and used more for tractor and other vehicle storage than for animals and hay. The white siding makes you squint, and as you step out of the car you can smell that very familiar smell of cow manure.

There are a few people milling about outside the entrance to the barn, and you notice then a girl about your age. It's a relief to see a fellow kid. It's funny, up until just recently you always thought of Chip as a kid.

She clearly is also happy to see you, and she comes right over to you with a kind smile.

"Hi!" she says. She sticks out her hand.

"Hi," you say and take it.

"Oz, this is Gabrielle, my daughter. Gabrielle, this is an old friend of mine, Oz," says Chip.

"I mean, not *that* old," she smiles as she shakes my hand firmly and then releases it.

"Long story," I say.

"Dad, I'm going to be late for school," she says, turning to Chip.

"Yeah, sorry, sweetie, Oz here held me up. I think you're going to have to skip today. Is that okay?" he asks.

Gabrielle nods. "I'd much rather help you out here, anyway. I'd rather be a hero than just read about them." You notice then she's carrying a big book with some kind of monster on the cover.

"That's my girl," says Chip. And it's so weird to think of him as a dad that you want to kind of laugh, but also you know it isn't the right moment for that. "Come on, let's get this meeting started." He looks over at some adults standing in the shade of one of the trees. "Let's get going!"

They nod, and all of you head into the shadows of the barn. There are a half dozen other adults already inside, sitting on some folding chairs and a bench along one wall. It doesn't look super organized or anything, but you're just happy you don't have to face this rabbit on your own anymore.

You and Gabrielle choose a pair of old barrels to sit on, and you both sit there dangling your legs and waiting for something to happen.

"What's going on?" you whisper to Gabrielle.

"We're just waiting for the leader. It's all good," she reassures you.

"Oh, I thought your dad was the leader."

She shakes her head.

Just as she does, a shadow materializes in the wide-open barn doorway. First, just a pair of legs, then a torso.

And then a pair of long tall ears.

The rabbit walks inside.

You want to make a run for it, and you wonder why everyone is just still sitting there like that.

"There it is!" says Gabrielle.

"Who?"

"The leader, of course!"

➤ **IF YOU SAY, "WHAT ARE YOU TALKING ABOUT, THAT'S THE RABBIT!" YOUR HEART PUMPING FAST, TURN TO PAGE 135.**

➤ **WHAT IS GOING ON? IF YOU SIT THERE AND STARE, SAYING NOTHING, TURN TO PAGE 140.**

You see those bunny ears you won in 1985 nestled in the bag, kind of hiding behind a book and your gym shorts. Just a little yellow fuzz poking out of the black void. You suddenly have a super crazy idea. What if you put them on? Maybe if you did that, the rabbit would think you are also a rabbit and leave you alone? It's a wacky idea, almost too wacky. Is this a situation where it's so crazy it just might work? Or, you know, just . . . crazy?

- **NOPE. TOO CRAZY. IF YOU DON'T PUT THEM ON AND CLOSE YOUR BAG, TURN TO PAGE 80.**
- **WHAT HAVE YOU GOT TO LOSE AT THIS POINT? MAYBE THE ONLY WAY TO FIGHT CRAZY IS WITH A LITTLE BIT OF CRAZY? IF YOU PUT THEM ON, TURN TO PAGE 138.**

Chip looks a little disappointed but he nods. "Yeah, that makes sense. I shouldn't have asked you, anyway. What kind of grown-up am I?" He laughs a bit to himself.

"It's weird thinking of you as a grown-up. I just saw you the other day as a kid," you say. It is kind of trippy to think.

Chip has this far-off look on his face now and he shakes his head slowly. "I'm trying to remember what I was like in 1985."

"You were really cool," you say.

"Yeah?"

"Oh yeah. And, well, I dunno."

Chip furrows his brow as he looks at you. "And what?"

"It's dumb, but you were also really nice to me."

"That's not dumb."

You shrug. "I guess not. It shouldn't be. But I feel like being nice isn't exactly something that's seen as cool, and you were both. It meant a lot. Not a lot of kids are nice to me."

"That's awful," says Chip. Now he's feeling sorry for you, and you didn't mean for that to happen. You feel pretty pathetic.

"Nah, it's fine. It's whatever. I like being a loner. But you and Mike were awesome and made this summer a lot better. Before . . . well, before the whole rabbit thing happened." You're now feeling more than just anger and fear about the rabbit—there's bitterness, too. You had a good thing going in 1985, and that rabbit totally ruined it.

"Mike! Oh man, I'd forgot he was still living here back then. Haven't heard from him in like . . . fifteen years."

"Fifteen years!" You haven't even been alive for that long! It's crazy to think you could have a whole friendship with someone and then also not see them for longer than a person had been existing.

"Yeah, he moved with his family the next year. He's in Boston now. Married. With kids."

"Whoa," you say.

Chip laughs.

"Crap, is that the time?" he says, suddenly looking at the clock on the dashboard. "Sorry, Oz. But I do have to go. Have a rabbit I have to take down."

"Totally!" You are not about to hold him back. There is nothing that matters more to you than the destruction of this rabbit. You quickly open your door and jump out into the street. "Good luck!" you say.

"Thanks, Oz!" he replies. "And hey, Oz?"

"Yeah?"

"I always thought you were pretty cool, too."

You grin at each other, and then you close the door. Chip speeds off and you watch him disappear around the corner.

You feel a really weird mix of feelings. Happy to have seen Chip again, kind of sad that he is all grown-up, scared that he might not defeat the rabbit, hopeful that he will. Time-travel is more complicated than you thought. It didn't just mess with space and time, but with your emotions as well.

You hear a sudden squeal of rubber on asphalt and you look up. A car is racing right for you. And not just any car—Dad's car. You can see the driver now. It's the rabbit.

You want to race to find Chip, to tell him the rabbit is right here and it's coming after him! As the car gets closer you realize what is happening a little too late. The rabbit is trying to kill *you* with the car. This has nothing to do with Chip! You try to run, but the rabbit is faster. Of course he is, he's driving a freaking car! He pushes the pedal to the metal and comes barreling toward you.

GAME OVER

>TO TRY AGAIN TURN TO PAGE 2

You pull the ears out from the depth of the bag and hold them in your hands. You don't remember them looking quite this ridiculous before. You suppose that in 1985 things tend to look less so because, well, everything is over-the-top. The bright neon, the huge hairstyles, the wild makeup choices that some of the girls had with the bright blue eyeshadow and super-pink lipstick. Everything is so gaudy and fake-looking. So a pair of yellow fuzzy bunny ears are practically understated. Also, when you're surrounded by flashing games and a wall of prizes, it all kind of just blends together.

Anyway, even if you feel a little silly doing this, you made a decision and you might as well try. Here goes, quite literally, nothing. You put them on and feel stupid. Really, really stupid.

Something sharp on each side of the plastic band just by the top of your ears suddenly pierces into your skull. Clamping onto it, hard.

It's shocking and sudden and you should cry out in pain, but for some reason you feel actually quite relaxed. Really relaxed. Super relaxed. It's like the stabbing into your flesh is a welcoming feeling, something you realize that you've always needed and now finally have.

You feel good.

You feel very bunny.

You are one with being a bunny.

Yes.

Yes, this is right, this is good.

You wander out of your room like you are floating, like your feet don't even touch the ground. You are looking for the rabbit and head to your parents' room. You discover the rabbit lying on the bed on top of the covers, with Mom next to it. They are watching some kind of documentary on bunnies on the TV. Oh, and look! Mom is wearing bunny ears, too!

You go and sit between them. Mom gives you a little squeeze

and you sink back into the pillows next to her. This is exactly what you wanted. To sit with your bunny family watching your bunny show. You look at the rabbit who looks at you, and even though its expression doesn't change, you know it is happy, too. Family night.

Together you all watch the show.

Forever.

GAME OVER

>TO TRY AGAIN TURN TO PAGE 2

As you step to the side, you accidentally step onto Jinx's milk bowl. Shoot! You totally forgot about it! You trip and fall onto the floor, spilling milk everywhere. The soggy wetness seeps into your socks and jeans. Jinx wakes up with a yowl and runs away to hide under your bed.

Great, just great. You've made a mess. But you're definitely not about to cry over spilt milk. Should you get changed before you try to sneak out? It seems like a lot of work to do in the moment. You decide to continue with your plan and push against the floor to stand up.

Before you can even get to your feet, the door to your room flings open. The rabbit is there! It's heard the commotion! It stares down at you. It knows you are up to something.

"Uh, hi?" you say, trying to sound as casual as possible.

It stares for a moment longer. Then suddenly it opens its mouth wide, so wide it unhinges its jaw like a snake. You still can't see the person in the suit, but you see rows of razor-sharp teeth. You cry out and raise your arms to save yourself, but they do nothing to protect you as the rabbit attacks.

GAME OVER

>TO TRY AGAIN TURN TO PAGE 2

"What are you talking about, Oz?" That's Chip. He's walking over to the rabbit, hand extended, as he turns and says that to you.

"Right there, it's . . . it's right there!" You point at the rabbit and it just stares back at you. For a creature that has zero expression on its face, it's amazing how well you can read it. Right now it appears satisfied, smug.

"Oz, man, are you okay?" asks Chip. He and the rabbit shake hands and Chip makes some kind of quiet apology to it. Now you know for sure that Chip is all grown-up: He's doing that dismissive thing adults do when they talk to each other to reassure each other that the kid that's acting weird is no big deal.

Except this is a huge deal.

You can't believe this is happening to you. Not here, not now.

"That's the rabbit," you say to Gabrielle. She's looking at you all weird, but she isn't being like the other grown-ups. She's actually listening.

"How can you tell?" she asks.

"I mean . . . look at it!" You gesture toward the figure and she looks.

"I don't get it."

"It's in a yellow rabbit costume, for crying out loud!"

Everyone is staring at you now. Even the people behind you, you can feel their eyes on you. You refuse to feel silly. You aren't losing your mind. After all, these people have gathered to take down the rabbit so surely they know he exists. You just have to get them to see it, somehow.

"I just see a guy," replied Gabrielle. She looks at you again and now she looks worried.

If even Gabrielle can't see it . . .

You feel a heavy hand on your shoulder and turn quickly. A woman in a dark green tank top and camouflage pants is looking at you severely. "Come with me," she says.

You look to Gabrielle, who doesn't seem to know what to do. She looks just as lost as you feel.

"Go with Ava," says Chip. "I'm sorry, Oz, but maybe time-travel has messed with your mind a little bit. We can't have you just having these outbursts when we have a mission to accomplish."

"What does that mean? Are you going to kill me?" You sit there, defiant, not ready to go anywhere.

Chip sputters and holds his hands up. "Kill you, what?! Of course not. We just need to keep you safe until the mission's done. Ava?"

The woman behind you grabs under your arms to lift you off the barrel, and she is very strong. You realize fighting it will only make things harder for you.

"Okay, okay, I'm coming," you say.

You get up and are led down to the other end of the barn, past all the people staring at you as you go. They think you're crazy. You worry a little bit that you are.

Ava takes you to a small storage room with no windows, just a single light bulb dangling from the center of the ceiling. You step inside. Well, this is fun.

"Sorry, kid, I'll come get you when we've completed the mission and take you home," she says. She closes the door behind her and you can hear her lock it with a clang on the other side.

Well, this is just fantastic, isn't it?

You wander around for a while, full of angry nervous energy, and finally you start to feel a little tired so you sit on the cold cement floor. You have no idea how much time has passed, if it's day or night. If they've left for the mission yet or not.

You just wait.

And wait.

And wait.

And then you hear the clang of the lock, and the door is opened slowly. You jump to your feet. You are so ready to explain and to just get the heck out of there.

In enters the rabbit.

You stumble backward, tripping over your feet. You fall hard onto that cement ground.

The rabbit looms over you and stares down. It raises its hand and ticks its finger back and forth the way you would at a naughty child. Then it opens its mouth wide. And wider. And wider. It unhinges its jaw, revealing rows of razor-sharp teeth. It lunges at you.

GAME OVER

>TO TRY AGAIN TURN TO PAGE 2

You pull the ears out from the depth of the bag and hold them in your hands. You don't remember them looking quite this ridiculous before. You suppose that in 1985 things tend to look less so because, well, everything is over-the-top. The bright neon, the huge hairstyles, the wild makeup choices that some of the girls had with the bright blue eyeshadow and super-pink lipstick. Everything is gaudy and fake-looking. So a pair of yellow fuzzy bunny ears are practically understated. Also, when you're surrounded by flashing games and a wall of prizes, it all kind of just blends together.

Anyway, even if you feel a little silly doing this, you made a decision and you might as well try. Here goes, quite literally, nothing. You put them on and feel stupid. Really, really stupid.

Something sharp on each side of the plastic band just by the top of your ears suddenly pierces into your skull. Clamping onto it—hard.

It's shocking and sudden and you should cry out in pain, but for some reason you feel actually quite relaxed. Really relaxed. Super relaxed. It's like the stabbing into your flesh is a welcoming feeling, something you realize that you've always needed and now finally have.

You feel good.

You feel very bunny.

You are one with being a bunny.

Yes.

Yes, this is right, this is good.

You get up and cross your room, floating almost like you're on a cloud of contentment. You go downstairs and sit at the table with Mom and the rabbit who have already started eating dinner. You smile at them. Mom is wearing bunny ears, too, and she smiles at you. And the rabbit . . . well, it can't exactly smile back, but you sense that it is smiling somewhere inside that costume.

You are a family.
A happy little bunny family.
This is the beginning of the rest of your life.

GAME OVER

>TO TRY AGAIN TURN TO PAGE 2

You sit there in stunned silence as Chip greets the rabbit, giving its hand a hearty shake. You continue to sit as Chip starts the meeting with the rabbit standing right beside him.

"Tonight we head to Jeff's and make a final stand," Chip is saying, but you barely hear it because all you can do is stare at the rabbit. And the rabbit definitely stares right back. It appears smug, like it's won something.

But it hasn't, you think to yourself. *Not yet*.

There is a huge cheer from the gathered crowd, including Gabrielle beside you, and you are quick to join in the applause.

Everyone is up on their feet now talking with one another, making plans for tonight, looking over maps, and finalizing weapons. You see several spiked baseball bats, some rope, pitchforks, which make sense seeing as you are in a barn, even if there are no animals. Chip is loading a rifle, which makes you feel uneasy.

But none of it will do anything if the adults don't understand that the rabbit is among them. It is literally leading them!

You need to talk to the only other kid in the room.

"Come with me," you whisper to Gabrielle as you grab her sleeve. She looks confused and concerned, but she follows you to a back corner behind a stack of oil drums.

"What's wrong?"

"You're going to think I'm crazy, but your leader is the rabbit." You peer through a crack in the stack of drums to keep an eye on it. The rabbit is "talking" to a woman in a green tank top and camouflage pants. Or rather she's talking to it—the rabbit is just standing and staring at her, expressionless.

Gabrielle joins you to peek. "How do you know?"

"Because it's dressed like a rabbit," you say. You look at her carefully. Does she seriously not see it?

"It looks like a man to me." You feel your heart sink. "But everything my dad's said about how clever the rabbit is, I wouldn't put it past it to disguise itself like this."

It feels so good to be believed you just want to give her a big hug. But that would be weird, considering you've only just met.

"I wonder why you can see it as its true self?" she adds.

You shake your head. "I have no idea. Maybe it's because I time-traveled."

"You time-traveled?" She looks seriously impressed.

"Yeah, that's how I met your dad."

"My dad?"

"Uh, yeah, we met in 1985 when I time-traveled. He was just a kid, our age." It doesn't feel like this is the time to explain all this.

"That's crazy!"

You shrug. It's weird, when everything in your life is crazy, it all starts to feel very normal.

"So," she says after you say nothing, "what should we do?"

➤ **IF BOTH OF YOU TAKE DOWN THE RABBIT, TURN TO PAGE 144.**

➤ **THERE'S NOTHING TO DO, IT'S TOO RISKY. IF IT'S BETTER TO JUST SEE WHAT HAPPENS, TURN TO PAGE 150.**

You take in a deep breath and release it very slowly through your mouth. You can do this. But you only have one shot at this (literally and metaphorically), so you need to be patient and take your time.

One foot in front of the other, step-by-step, you carefully walk over to Dad's side of the bed. Being this close to the rabbit makes your stomach clench and your pulse quicken. You can also now smell that weird, stale, moldy scent that seems to live in that terrible matted yellow costume. It makes you a little dizzy and nauseated, but you are focused.

You raise your hand above your head and aim the syringe right at the rabbit's heart. Or at least where you hope a heart is. Does such a monster have a heart? Literally? Metaphorically?

You bring your hand down fast, but suddenly the rabbit has you by the wrist and sits up in one quick motion, relieving you of the syringe with its other hand.

You cry out and try to wrench your arm free, but it has you tight in its grasp. You pull and pull, and the rabbit tackles you off the bed and onto the floor. You are pinned beneath it. It's the rabbit's turn to pull its hand back high over your chest with the syringe.

"No!" you cry out, but it's too late. You feel the sharp stabbing pain of the syringe piercing your chest. You open your eyes wide and gasp, and then you feel a heaviness overtake you.

You close your eyes to sleep.

You never wake up.

GAME OVER

>TO TRY AGAIN TURN TO PAGE 2

Slow and steady wins the race, that's what they say, right? You realize in that moment the saying actually comes from the old fable about the tortoise and the hare. About them racing and how even though the hare is quick, the tortoise's slow determination makes him the winner. Well, how perfect is that then? You'll be the tortoise to defeat the rabbit!

You just need to take the stairs one by one, step-by-step and you'll be outside in no time. Shouldn't be too hard. You hope.

But as you take that first step down, you hear an all-too-familiar creak. It's funny how a creaky staircase is meaningless to the point that you totally forget it's a thing, and then suddenly it can become literally life and death. You turn your head quickly to see if the rabbit heard you. There's no one there. Just a deep blackness of shadow.

You release a sigh and take another slow step. The creak starts the second you place a toe on it. You complete the step, the creak finally finishes, and you stand there perfectly still, waiting for the inevitable attack.

Nothing.

You dare to look over your shoulder.

There in the dark is a familiar silhouette.

The rabbit!

You turn and face downstairs! What do you do?!

➤ **IF YOU RUN FOR IT, TURN TO PAGE 147.**

➤ **IF YOU FREEZE IN PLACE, TURN TO PAGE 148.**

"We have to take down the rabbit. We can't let it manipulate all these people. Whatever it is planning, it's evil. I know that for sure."

Gabrielle nods. "I agree. But how do we take it down?"

You look around the room from your hiding spot and see the rope on the ground with the other weapons. "Maybe we can trap it, and then we can figure it out from there. Maybe if we tie it up, we can convince your dad and everyone else that this is the rabbit. It'll buy us some time at least."

"Yeah, that makes sense. Plus, I don't think I'm really up to killing anyone."

You agree, that's kind of a crazy thought, and even though this rabbit has killed a bunch of kids and done something terrible to your dad, you just don't think you are ready for that, either.

Maybe in self-defense, but even then. The idea of ending a life is super heavy and just a bit too real for you to even contemplate this carefully.

"So let's get some rope, and then we need to find a moment when the rabbit is alone," you say. "But we'd better have the rope at the ready."

"Totally."

You make your way from your little hiding spot back out into the open. You're trying to be as chill as possible, just looking at everything everyone is doing. You wander over to the woman in green and look down at the blueprints of Jeff's Pizza she is studying. You see the ball pit in the corner. "That should be our primary focus," you say.

She looks at you.

"That's where the rabbit comes from. That's the portal to another time."

She looks at you even harder.

"Just . . . uh . . . trust me on that one," you say and slowly back away from her. You see her turn back to the blueprints and make a mark on the spot you were pointing out with a pen. Well, at least she's listening to you, even if she thinks you're crazy.

You wander over to Chip and his weapons. You pick up a bat. It's weighed down with the barbed wire wrapped around it. You are reminded how terrible you are at gym class.

"You okay?" asks Chip.

"A little nervous, honestly." You put down the bat. You pick up a length of rope. "I don't want, like, a weapon or anything."

"And I wouldn't let you have one, anyway."

You can't help but laugh. "It's weird to have you acting like an adult with me. Protective, you know?"

Chip grimaces. "I guess. Just remember I didn't actually time-travel. I've lived the last few decades of my life in real time. I've grown up."

There's something harsh in the way he says "grown up," but you can't tell if he's mocking you or he's mad about getting older. You can't really tell what's going on at all anymore.

"Totally," you reply.

You back off but take the rope with you.

You meet back up with Gabrielle who's managed to grab some duct tape.

"Awesome," you say.

"Yeah, I figured duct tape is useful for all kinds of situations."

"Absolutely."

You smile at each other.

"Now what?" she asks.

"Now we wait."

And that's exactly what you do. You wait and you watch until you're starting to feel a little bored. You understand why in the movies, cops drink so much coffee on their stakeouts. You definitely need artificial help to stay vigilant when nothing is happening.

But finally you see the rabbit cross away from the group and head toward an exit on the side of the building.

You nudge Gabrielle, who nods back. The two of you stick to the shadows and creep along the edge of the barn, following it. You hold the rope so tight in your hands you can feel it scratching away the skin on your palms.

You can do this.

You can do this.

You and Gabrielle follow the rabbit outside to a small dirt courtyard. It's empty except for a few piles of bricks in the corner.

The rabbit's back is to you, and you wonder for a moment what it's thinking. Does it even think?

No, stop it, you have to act! The time is now!

"Now!" you shout.

You rush at the rabbit and aim for its lower half. It's too big to take down on your own, but if you can unbalance it and have it fall, well, that's a good start.

You and Gabrielle tackle the rabbit together and it falls hard face-first onto the ground. You quickly reach the rope around its neck, but the head suddenly turns 180 degrees to stare right back up at you, causing you to flinch.

That brief moment sets you off-balance and suddenly the rabbit has overpowered the two of you and you are the ones now on the dusty ground. You lie there in horror as you see its jaw unhinge and mouth open wide, producing a set of razor-sharp teeth.

You and Gabrielle scream at the same time.

Your screams are silenced by the slicing of teeth into flesh.

GAME OVER

>TO TRY AGAIN TURN TO PAGE 2

You race down the stairs. Forget being a tortoise, it's hare all the way now! But, of course, you manage to prove the saying true. In your haste and speed, you and your body are totally out of sync and you trip over yourself. You fall hard and then tumble down to the bottom. Everything hurts but not nearly as bad as the feeling of the razor-sharp teeth that sink deep into your flesh. The rabbit has you in its grasp.

GAME OVER

>TO TRY AGAIN TURN TO PAGE 2

You stand perfectly still. You hold your body so tight that you can feel it start to ache from the effort. You're nervous that you are so stiff you might keel over and tumble down the stairs. You grip the railing tightly—you will not move.

You will not move an inch.

You are so determined you hold your breath, you will your pulse to slow down even as it races on without your permission. You are a statue. You are furniture.

You hear the rabbit slowly move toward you. It is being careful, methodical. Taking steps one by one, slow and steady, winning the race. Of course the race was won by the tortoise, not the hare. Maybe that gives you an advantage? After all, you are the tortoise in this situation.

You hear it come up right behind you. You can smell that musty-moldy smell from that matted yellow costume. You can hear it breathing. The fact that it can breathe at all unsettles you. Either a person truly is wearing this costume, which is a terrifying thought. Or this is a living, breathing monster that looks like someone in a mascot costume—which is also petrifying. Either way, whatever this thing is, it seems to be alive.

You stand there for what feels like hours. Finally, you hear the rabbit start to back away up the stairs, and the breathing sounds vanish. With effort, you can hear the sound of retreating footsteps.

And yet you stay still. Just to be safe. Just for a moment longer.

Finally, after probably a little too long, you release a sigh of relief.

You are suddenly grabbed from behind by a pair of yellow arms. They are the last things you ever feel or see.

GAME OVER

>TO TRY AGAIN TURN TO PAGE 2

You have no time to waste crossing the entire house. You'll just fling open the door superfast and make a run for it! That's all there is to it!

You take in a deep breath and hold it. You reach for the doorknob and turn it slowly until you hear the click of it unlocking. It sounds so loud it almost feels like it echoes. You need to speed up, you need to fling open the door, just like you'd planned. Just do it. *Just do it!* You yank open the door quickly, and the squeak it makes is so loud you almost jump at the sound.

Did the rabbit hear, too?

You turn to see if it did, just as it launches itself at you, jaw unhinged like a snake with rows of razor-sharp teeth. You feel sharp pain and cry out. It's unlike anything you've felt before.

GAME OVER

>TO TRY AGAIN TURN TO PAGE 2

"We can't do anything. The adults won't believe us—trust me, I've tried. I think we just have to wait and see what happens. Hopefully the rabbit will slip up," you say. It's unsatisfying but you know it's the right thing. It's not like you can just take on this crazy rabbit by yourselves. And you are in a room with a bunch of adults and weapons . . . surely at some point that might help?

"Yeah, and it would be dangerous. I mean, I'm not even supposed to be here. I was supposed to be at school," replies Gabrielle.

"Yeah, me too." And for some reason even though it's not the point of everything happening, you ask, "What school do you go to?"

"We just moved, so it was going to be my first day. Westbrook Middle School."

You can't help but laugh. "That's my school."

"Oh, funny! I guess we would have met there, huh?"

You nod. And you wonder if in a different universe what would have happened if you'd just met her as a friend during a normal day. Under normal circumstances.

How weird "normal" seems now.

"Let's just wait it out and see what happens," you say. "But let's make sure not to go anywhere alone. We don't want it to corner us or anything. I think we're safe as long as there are other people around."

"Makes sense."

So that's what you do.

You make your way from your little hiding spot back out into the open. You're trying to be as chill as possible, just looking at everything everyone is doing. You wander over to the woman in green and look down at the blueprints of Jeff's Pizza she's studying. You see the ball pit in the corner. "That should be our primary focus," you say.

She looks at you.

"That's where the rabbit comes from. That's the portal to another time."

She looks at you even harder.

"Just . . . uh . . . trust me on that one," you say and slowly back away from her. You see her turn back to the blueprints and make a mark on the spot you pointed out with a pen. Well, at least she's listening to you, even if she thinks you're crazy.

You wander over to Chip and his weapons. You pick up a bat. It's weighed down with the barbed wire wrapped around it. You are reminded how terrible you are at gym class.

"You okay?" asks Chip.

"A little nervous, honestly." You put down the bat. You pick up a length of rope. "I don't want, like, a weapon or anything."

"And I wouldn't let you have one, anyway."

You can't help but laugh. "It's weird you acting like an adult with me. Protective, you know?"

Chip grimaces. "I guess. Just remember I didn't actually time-travel, I've lived the last few decades in real time. I've grown up."

There's something harsh in the way he says "grown up," but you can't tell if he is telling you off or he's mad about getting older. You can't really tell what's going on at all anymore.

"Totally," you reply. You put down the rope and wander over to another group of adults sitting and talking in a small circle. You feel safe keeping your back to the wall surrounded by adults. But you always keep an eye on the rabbit's whereabouts. You think it is probably doing likewise with you.

Time passes and the sun starts to set. You can't believe you've been here all day. There's a shift in the energy then, and you sense that the time is coming soon. Time for action!

"All right, everyone, let's do this!" Chip announces loudly to the group.

Everyone is up on their feet, finalizing plans and grabbing weapons. Gabrielle runs over to you and looks at you with wide eyes. Yup, it's happening. What is happening . . . what will happen . . . that's a whole other question.

"Oz, Gabrielle, you're with me," says Chip, approaching. "You'll stay in the car."

"Dad, we can help!" insists Gabrielle, but you're not exactly upset to be left out of things.

"No, Gabrielle."

As you follow Chip to the car, you run a little to step in next to him. "Hey, can you make sure you look for my dad?" you ask.

Chip nods.

"It's just, he's in the ball pit, somewhere. It's bigger than you think it is, it's like a whole pool or maybe even the size of a lake. You need to really search."

Chip holds open the back-seat door for you, and Gabrielle hops in. He isn't making eye contact with you. "Chip, dude," you say. Chip looks down at you now. "Please. My dad."

He looks at you and you don't exactly know what he's thinking. Finally, he nods. "After we take care of the rabbit, we'll find your dad."

"Thanks."

"Now get in."

You jump in beside Gabrielle. The woman in the green tank top gets in the passenger side up front and Chip is in the driver's seat. Soon you are leading a caravan of cars and trucks down the twisting driveway. In the dark, every new bend in the road that materializes in the glow of the headlights feels like a threat, like something is ready to jump out at you. You turn around in your seat and squint through the headlights of the car behind you. You can't make out much, but you can see the silhouette of the rabbit in the passenger seat. It is just sitting there. Just staring forward. Like it always does.

You turn around again.

"You okay?" asks Gabrielle quietly.

You nod, but you so aren't. You have a sinking feeling that this is all some kind of trap. That you are all doomed.

You arrive in town and pull up in front of Jeff's Pizza. The plan starts the moment the engines stop. Everyone barrels out of their cars and into Jeff's, weapons raised.

"We know you're in there!" Chip calls out.

You watch from inside the car as the rabbit walks inside after him. No, this is too much. This is too dangerous. You can't just let this happen.

You fling open your passenger side door and race after Chip.

"Oz!" you hear Gabrielle cry. You know you're supposed to stay behind, but you have to do something, anything.

You walk into the restaurant and see a very surprised Jeff standing behind his counter. He makes eye contact with you for a moment and you don't know what to say.

"Jeff, get into the kitchen," orders Chip.

Jeff kind of just stands there in his usual kind of way.

"Now!" Chip turns and yells at him. That definitely sparks action in the pizza chef, and Jeff sprints into the kitchen.

"Where is it?" asks Ava in the green tank top. She's looking around, alert and holding her weapon in front of her. She must have some kind of army training or something.

"It's right there," you want to say as you watch the rabbit watch them. It's just standing there, over by its usual door, that stupid door that the mascot loves to hover around. But they can't see it.

You look around at everyone, willing someone, *anyone*, to notice the rabbit. Your eyes fall onto the ball pit. Wait. What are you doing? You realize suddenly that this is your moment. Let them all hunt for the rabbit while you save Dad!

You rush over to the ball pit and jump in without pause. You sink into the giant pool of balls and somehow they feel oddly comforting. They are the one familiar thing in a day of insanity. You reach around into the balls, trying to feel for Dad. He's got to be here somewhere—*he's got to be.*

You feel something hard with your hand. A shoe! Attached to a foot! You reach farther . . . attached to a leg! It has to be Dad. You've found him!

There is a sudden bloodcurdling scream, and you pull yourself up out of the pit to see what has happened. To your horror, the rabbit has attacked Chip, biting his head right off! Chip's body falls limp to the side. Ava screams again and this time fires off her weapon just as two other men rush the rabbit from behind with baseball bats. The rabbit whirls and flails, and you stand up in the ball pit. You are overwhelmed by the chaos, and another shot rings out. Suddenly you feel something warm spread across your middle, and you look down. You see blood and you reach to hold your stomach. The blood oozes around your fingers.

More shots fired, more chaos. You slip down into the pit. You are in shock. Nothing hurts. You lie back. You let the balls cover you for good.

GAME OVER

>TO TRY AGAIN TURN TO PAGE 2

The ball pit becomes an infinite pool, colorful balls upon balls upon balls. There is no up, there is no down, there is no escape. The world is just plastic balls now. You sink and sink. You try to swim up to the surface as you have before, but there is no surface. Just oblivion in the form of plastic balls in every direction around you.

Your body relaxes into the realization. You feel nothing but hopelessness, but in that feeling there is a sense of freedom. You don't care. You don't care about anything. About yourself, about Dad, about the rabbit.

You are free from thought and worries and even boredom.

You are free because you are trapped.

You are trapped.

Floating in your sea of hard plastic and cloying color.

GAME OVER

>TO TRY AGAIN TURN TO PAGE 2

You remember Theseus, and how he had his friend, Princess Ariadne, to help him. How you wish you had one now! You feel certain Gabrielle would actually come to your aid. You only just met, but she was really nice and enthusiastic about everything you had to say. She seems to genuinely enjoy your company. Besides, she loves reading about heroes—you bet she wouldn't mind being one. A Hercules or a Theseus or an Ariadne.

And then you remember the string. *String!* Of course!

You use all the strength that is left within you and wallop the rabbit in the face with your free hand. It's hardly a hard punch, but it's enough that it releases its grip on your arm. You lunge at the netting around the ball pit to grab it and pull it toward you. You will entangle the rabbit with the string!

The rabbit catches you by your other arm and wrenches at it hard, breaking it with an easy snap as if it was nothing more than a twig. You scream out in pain, your head swims, you feel bile rise up in your throat. You release the netting and fall to the ground useless and ashamed.

The rabbit rises up before you and looks at you one last time.

"Please don't," you ask futilely.

It stares at you, with pity maybe? Like it is disappointed in your attempt to defeat it. Then it opens its mouth, unhinging its jaw again in that horrible snakelike fashion. You have nothing left in you to defend yourself. You close your eyes and brace yourself for the attack.

It chomps down on you, and the last thing you remember is a piercing white-hot pain.

GAME OVER

>TO TRY AGAIN TURN TO PAGE 2

There is really nothing that indicates a better route, no smells wafting from one direction, no noises to avoid. It's just luck, just chance. Whatever you choose will either be the correct choice or the wrong choice.

So you choose left.

You crawl along the vent and you feel it shaking as the other kids follow behind you. It's a lot of shaking. Almost *too* much. Just as you suddenly wonder whether vents are meant to carry the weight of six kids, the floor beneath you gives way and you all tumble out of the vent into the kitchen below you.

And right on top of the rabbit.

There's a heavy thud as its head meets the concrete, and you jump up, ready to fight or run away, but notice the rabbit's body is super still. As the kids clamber off it, you realize that the rabbit is unconscious.

Oh. That's good. That's very good! Now you just have to . . .

. . . do . . . something . . .

Your mind is feeling a little weird, and that's when you notice the room is growing foggy. You look around and up and see that a pipe in the ceiling is spewing some kind of gas. You are feeling pretty dizzy now, and you hear a *thud*. And another *thud*. You turn to see the kids passing out around you, dropping like flies.

Well, that's not good.

Your eyes roll back into your head and then . . .

Blackness.

Until you regenerate back in front of the arcade game. You are still a little dizzy and confused, but you're not sure if it's because of the gas or the regeneration. It takes you a moment to realize what's happened.

Oh. I can't die. Or maybe you only have a certain number of lives? But it's a game. *I'm in a game*, you tell yourself.

The pain was real, though. You wince when remembering it.

You're not sure how many times you want to be murdered by a rabbit mascot.

Well, you're back at the start now. And you still need to escape from this game. You really don't have much of a choice, so you might as well try again!

➤ TURN BACK TO PAGE 31

There is really nothing that indicates a better route, no smells wafting from one direction, no noises to avoid. It's just luck, just chance. Whatever you choose will either be the correct choice or the wrong choice.

So you choose right.

You turn and start to crawl down that vent, and the kids follow you dutifully. Your hands and knees are getting sore, and so is your back. That you can feel things in this game freaks you out. You really need to win this thing. You don't want to know what's going to happen if you don't.

Finally, you see daylight far down the vent. An exit! Thank goodness!

But you also hear a noise from directly below you. Your moment of relief is replaced by panic as you look down through the small holes in the vent shaft. There's the rabbit. It is walking directly below you.

- **IF YOU GO EXTRA FAST TO REACH THE EXIT, TURN TO PAGE 160.**
- **IF YOU FREEZE IN PLACE, HOLDING YOUR BREATH, WAITING FOR THE RABBIT TO GO AWAY, TURN TO PAGE 73.**

You speed down the vent as fast as you can, and feel from the vibrations behind you that the other kids are doing the same. You really hope the vent doesn't collapse under the activity. You reach the light and glance down through the holes below you just to make sure the rabbit isn't somehow beneath you. It's nowhere to be seen so you quickly jump out of the vent, landing a little harder than you'd like on your feet on the floor. Actually, now that you look up to see the other kids jumping down, you're kind of impressed how high up it is and with yourself for jumping at all, not just for the excellent landing.

You have managed to jump down into the main part of the restaurant. You are so grateful you chose to go right, you almost want to cry. Now you need to get *out* of here!

You turn to the kids, but one of them has taken this moment to sit at the birthday table. He's smiling and looks not at all concerned about the rabbit. Of course *you* are. You very much are concerned.

"Can we have some cake?" the box above his head reads.

Are you kidding me? We don't have time for this! The rabbit could come upon them at any moment!

"Yes—we want cake!" A text box appears over all the other kids' heads.

Guys, come on!

They all sit at the table.

Priorities, people!

Suddenly the back door to the hall flings open and the rabbit is right there. It makes its way slowly but steadily toward all of you by the birthday table, heading right for the kids!

You gesture wildly at the kids, but they just sit there, smiling at you.

- IF YOU TRY TO GIVE THEM SOME CAKE SO THEY'LL LISTEN TO YOU, TURN TO PAGE 83.
- NO WAY, YOU WILL NOT LET THEM EAT CAKE. IF YOU RUSH OVER AND PHYSICALLY PULL THEM OUT OF THE CHAIRS, INSISTING YOU RUN OUT THE FRONT DOOR AWAY FROM THE RABBIT, TURN TO PAGE 163.

A map is not in this game. You are the one who must live (?) with your shame. You know what they say: Cheaters don't win. But those who might try make the yellow rabbit grin.

> THE GAME HAS CRASHED.

GAME OVER

>TO TRY AGAIN TURN TO PAGE 2

This is no time for cake! You are insistent and start to pull the kid closest to you off his chair. Even though you can't speak, the kids seem to understand you by now. They all get up and follow you as you book it for the front door. You don't even look over your shoulder. You hope the rabbit is still doing that strange slow-walking thing, but you can hear heavy footsteps behind you and are pretty sure it has discovered how to run. You're pretty sure it's chasing you!

Well, run as fast as you can, rabbit, because we win!

You burst out of the restaurant into the welcoming daylight.

Only . . . no . . . it's not daylight. It's just an empty white space. Above, around, and below you. Your whole body feels weightless and you realize you are floating. You see the kids are floating, too. Oh! And there's the rabbit! It made it outside, too, evidently. And it's also floating. You are all a little stunned at this turn of events. Your legs float up and you can see your feet. You notice the little pixels that make up your body seem wider apart than they were before. You look at your hands. Yes, you can definitely see white breaking through your skin. The pixels float wider and wider apart, and you realize that you are crumbling into little pieces. Disintegrating pixel by pixel. The kids are disintegrating now. The rabbit is as well. Your pixels float apart and mingle with everyone else's pixels. It all starts to mix together. You are no longer you. You are one with the pixels. With the whiteness. With the other kids. With the rabbit.

It is not exactly a feeling of peace.

But it is a feeling that this is right.

This is your forever.

Forever.

Until you regenerate back in front of the arcade game. You are a little dizzy and confused. It takes you a moment to realize what's happened.

Oh. I can't die. Or maybe you only have a certain number of lives? But it's a game. *I'm in a game*, you tell yourself.

Then again, you're not sure how many times you want to want to die.

Well, you're back at the start now. And you still need to escape from this game. You really don't have much of a choice, so you might as well try again!

➤ TURN BACK TO PAGE 31

Once again, you gesture for the kids to follow you. They don't seem happy about it at all. "Are you sure?" appears in a text box above them and you nod. You are sure. You are also sure that the longer you wait to do this, the more chances you all have of being seen by the rabbit!

"Come on!" you say. Or sing. Or muzak-talk. Or whatever it is that makes it impossible to talk in the game. You'd love a text box of your own at this point.

The kids are reluctant, but they walk up to you and you are relieved.

You turn back to the restaurant. The rabbit still is facing away from you.

Follow me, kids, you think to yourself. And then you step into the restaurant. You are literally on your tiptoes, and you turn to check on the kids and notice they are also on their toes. Well, that's something, at least. You hunch a little to make yourself smaller, and they do, too, and all six of you, as quietly and quickly as you can, make your way through the restaurant.

Your peripheral vision warns you of another text box and you glance up. "It's coming!"

What?

You turn and see the rabbit is barreling toward you all.

"Run!" you sing-speak.

But the kids don't need to be told that. Everyone scatters and you run toward the arcade games. The rabbit has decided to follow you, and since you feel responsible for these kids now, you kind of don't mind. Better you than them!

What you *do* mind is when it distends its pixelated jaw and envelops your torso with its mouth, piercing your flesh with its sharp pixel teeth. You try to scream out, but again it's just musical notes. As you die, you watch as the rabbit turns its attention to the kids, picking them off one by one.

You are a failure.

You are ashamed.

Everything fades to blackness.

A perpetual night.

Forever dead.

Until you regenerate back in front of the arcade game. You are a little dizzy and confused. It takes you a moment to realize what's happened.

Oh. I can't die. Or maybe you only have a certain number of lives? But it's a game. *I'm in a game*, you tell yourself.

The pain was real, though. You wince when remembering it. You're not sure how many times you want to be torn to shreds by a rabbit mascot.

Well, you're back at the start now. And you still need to escape from this game. You really don't have much of a choice, so you might as well try again!

GAME OVER

>TO TRY AGAIN TURN TO PAGE 2

You lead the kids as quickly as you can to the back exit of the building. You push hard against the door and it doesn't budge. You try again. And again. And again.

Crap.

You have no choice. You have to try to exit through the restaurant.

You make your way back along the hallway, past the storage room, to the door back into the restaurant, and carefully open it, looking into the space. You see the rabbit standing by the birthday table. You see the exit to the outside on your right. You can do this. You *have* to do this.

➤ **TURN TO PAGE 165.**

ABOUT THE AUTHORS

SCOTT CAWTHON is the author of the bestselling video game series *Five Nights at Freddy's*, and while he is a game designer by trade, he is first and foremost a storyteller at heart. He is a graduate of The Art Institute of Houston and lives in Texas with his family.

ADRIENNE KRESS is a Toronto-born actor and writer. Her books include the award-winning and internationally published novels *Alex and the Ironic Gentleman*, *Timothy and the Dragon's Gate*, and *Hatter Madigan: Ghost in the H.A.T.B.O.X.* (with bestselling author Frank Beddor), as well as the steampunk novel *The Friday Society* and the gothic novel *Outcast*. She is also the author of the quirky three-book series The Explorers. Adrienne's first foray into writing horror came with her work on the *Bendy and the Ink Machine* novels, but as an actor she has had the pleasure of being creepy in such horror films as *Devil's Mile* and *Wolves*. And she took great pleasure in getting to haunt teenagers in SyFy's *Neverknock*.

NOTES